# SIMPLY WINDOWS® 7

*by Paul McFedries*

## WILEY

First published under the title Windows 7 Simplified, ISBN 978-0-470-50387-4 by **Wiley Publishing, Inc.,** 10475 Crosspoint Boulevard, Indianapolis, IN 46256

Copyright © 2010 by Wiley Publishing, Inc., Indianapolis, Indiana
This edition first published 2010.

Copyright © 2010 for the EMEA adaptation: John Wiley & Sons, Ltd.

*Registered office*

John Wiley & Sons Ltd, The Atrium, Southern Gate, Chichester, West Sussex, PO19 8SQ, United Kingdom

For details of our global editorial offices, for customer services and for information about how to apply for permission to reuse the copyright material in this book please see our website at www.wiley.com.

Wiley also publishes its books in a variety of electronic formats. Some content that appears in print may not be available in electronic books.

All prices correct at time of going to press. Please check appropriate website for current details.

All website information was correct at the time of going to press. Websites do constantly update their privacy settings and policies. Please check the relevant website homepage to find their current policies.

ISBN 978-0-470-71133-0

A catalogue record for this book is available from the British Library.

Printed in Italy by Printer Trento S.r.l.

## Permissions

Microsoft product screenshots reprinted with permission from Microsoft Corporation.

Corbis Digital Stock
Digital Vision
PhotoDisc/Getty Images
Purestock

# Publisher's Acknowledgements

Some of the people who helped bring this book to market include the following:

## Editorial and Production

VP Consumer and Technology Publishing Director: Michelle Leete

Associate Director – Book Content Management: Martin Tribe

Associate Publisher: Chris Webb

Executive Commissioning Editor: Birgit Gruber

Publishing Assistant: Ellie Scott

Production Manager: Amie Jackowski Tibble

Project Editor: Juliet Booker

Development Editor: Shena Deuchars

## Marketing:

Senior Marketing Manager: Louise Breinholt

Marketing Executive: Chloe Tunnicliffe

## Composition Services:

Layout: Andrea Hornberger

Graphics: Ana Carrillo

Indexer: Potomac Indexing, LLC

Series Designer: Patrick Cunningham

## About the Author

**Paul McFedries** is a full-time technical writer. Paul has been authoring computer books since 1991 and he has more than 60 books to his credit. Paul's books have sold more than three million copies worldwide. These books include the Wiley titles *Windows 7 Visual Quick Tips, Switching to a Mac Portable Genius, iPhone 3G Portable Genius, Teach Yourself VISUALLY Office 2008 for Mac,* and *Internet Simplified.* Paul is also the proprietor of Word Spy (www.wordspy.com and twitter.com/wordspy), a Web site that tracks new words and phrases as they enter the language. Paul invites you to drop by his personal Web site at www.mcfedries.com or to follow him on Twitter at twitter.com/paulmcf.

## Author's Acknowledgements

It goes without saying that writers focus on text, and I certainly enjoyed focusing on the text that you'll read in this book. However, this book is more than just the usual collection of words and phrases. A quick thumb-through of the pages will show you that this book is also chock-full of images, from sharp screen shots to fun and informative illustrations. Those colorful images sure make for a beautiful book, and that beauty comes from a lot of hard work by Wiley's immensely talented group of designers and layout artists. Of course, what you read in this book must also be accurate, logically presented, and free of errors. Ensuring all of this was an excellent group of editors that included project editor Sarah Hellert, copy editor Scott Tullis, and technical editor Vince Averello. Thanks to all of you for your exceptional competence and hard work. Thanks, as well, to acquisitions editor Jody Lefevere for asking me to write this book.

# How to Use This Book

Do you look at the pictures in a book or magazine before anything else? Would you rather be shown instead of read about how to do something? Then this book is for you. Opening *Simply Windows 7* allows you to read less and learn more about the Windows operating system.

## Who Needs This Book

This book is for a reader who has never used this particular technology or application. It is also for more computer literate individuals who want to expand their knowledge of the different features that Windows has to offer.

## Using the Mouse

This book uses the following conventions to describe the actions you perform when using the mouse:

### Click

Press your left mouse button once. You generally click your mouse on something to select something on the screen.

### Double-click

Press your left mouse button twice. Double-clicking something on the computer screen generally opens whatever item you have double-clicked.

### Right-click

Press your right mouse button. When you right-click anything on the computer screen, the program displays a shortcut menu containing commands specific to the selected item.

### Click and Drag, and Release the Mouse

Move your mouse pointer and hover it over an item on the screen. Press and hold down the left mouse button. Now, move the mouse to where you want to place the item and then release the button. You use this method to move an item from one area of the computer screen to another.

## The Conventions in This Book

A number of typographic and layout styles have been used throughout *Simply Windows 7* to distinguish different types of information.

### Bold

Bold type represents the names of commands and options that you interact with. Bold type also indicates text and numbers that you must type into a dialog box or window.

### Italics

Italic words introduce a new term and are followed by a definition.

### Numbered Steps

You must perform the instructions in numbered steps in order to successfully complete a section and achieve the final results.

### Bulleted Steps

These steps point out various optional features. You do not have to perform these steps; they simply give additional information about a feature. Steps without bullets tell you what the program does in response to your following a numbered step. For example, if you click a menu command, a dialog box may appear or a window may open. The step text may also tell you what the final result is when you follow a set of numbered steps.

### Notes

Notes give additional information. They may describe special conditions that may occur during an operation. They may warn you of a situation that you want to avoid – for example, the loss of data. A note may also cross reference a related area of the book. A cross reference may guide you to another chapter or another section within the current chapter.

### Icons and Buttons

Icons and buttons are graphical representations within the text. They show you exactly what you need to click to perform a step.

You can easily identify the tips or warnings in any section by looking for the Tip and Warning icons. Tips offer additional information, including tips, hints, and tricks. You can use the tip information to go beyond what you have learned in the steps. Warnings tell you about solutions to common problems and general pitfalls to avoid.

# Table of Contents

# 3 CREATING AND EDITING DOCUMENTS 36

# 4 WORKING WITH IMAGES 56

## 5 PLAYING MUSIC AND OTHER MEDIA 70

## 6 WORKING WITH FILES 88

# CONTENTS

# GETTING STARTED WITH WINDOWS 7

Are you ready to learn about Windows 7? In this chapter, you learn a few basic techniques and concepts that will help you get comfortable with Windows. These topics include starting Windows 7, understanding what you can do with Windows 7, and taking a tour of the Windows 7 screen. You also learn how to use a mouse with Windows 7, use the Windows 7 Help system, and activate your copy of Windows 7. The chapter closes by showing you how to shut down your system when you are finished using it.

# START WINDOWS 7

When you turn on your computer, Windows 7 starts automatically, but you may have to navigate the Welcome screen along the way. You use the Welcome screen to log in to Windows 7 using the user account and password you configured when you first set up your computer.

If this is the first time you are starting your computer, you will have to run through a series of configuration steps. These steps configure your main user account, your desktop background, and a few security options. You should select the default options to ensure your computer remains secure and up to date.

① Turn on your computer.

The Windows 7 Welcome screen appears.

**Note:** *If your version of Windows 7 is configured with just a single user and no password, then you bypass the Welcome screen and go directly to the desktop.*

② Click the icon that corresponds to your Windows 7 user name.

Windows 7 prompts you to enter your password.

**Note:** *If you are the only user on your computer, Windows 7 prompts you for your password right away, so you can skip Step **2**.*

Type your password.

**Note:** *The password characters appear as dots as you type them so that no one else can read your password.*

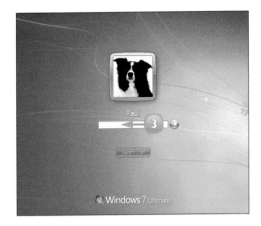

4 Click the **Go** arrow () or press Enter.

The Windows 7 desktop appears after a few moments.

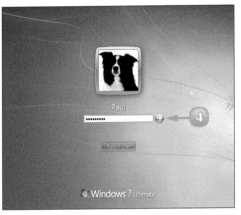

 **If you forget your password, click the Go arrow (🡒) and OK to see the hint – a word or phrase to jog your memory.**

# WHAT YOU CAN DO WITH WINDOWS 7

Windows 7 is an operating system that contains a collection of tools, programs, and resources. You do not do anything directly with Windows 7 itself. Instead, you use its tools and programs to perform tasks, including getting your work done, creating pictures, editing photos, playing music, surfing the World Wide Web, exchanging e-mail messages, and more. Here is a sample of what you can do with them.

## Get Work Done

With Windows 7, you can run programs that enable you to get your work done more efficiently, such as a word processor for writing memos and letters, a spreadsheet for making calculations, and a database for storing information. Windows 7 comes with some of these programs (such as the WordPad program you learn about in Chapter 3), and you can purchase and install others separately.

## Create and Edit Pictures

Windows 7 comes with a lot of features that let you work with images. You can create your own pictures from scratch, import images from a scanner or digital camera, or download images from the Internet. After you create or acquire an image, you can edit it, print it, or send it via e-mail. You learn about these and other picture tasks in Chapter 4.

## Play Music and Other Media

Windows 7 has treats for your ears as well as your eyes. You can listen to audio CDs, play digital sound and video clips, watch DVD movies, tune in to Internet radio stations, and copy audio files to a recordable CD. You learn about these multimedia tasks in Chapter 5.

## Get on the Internet

Windows 7 makes connecting to the Internet easy. And after you are on the Net, Windows 7 has all the tools you need to get the most out of your experience. For example, you can use Internet Explorer to surf the World Wide Web (see Chapter 8) and Windows Live Mail to send and receive e-mail (see Chapter 9).

# THE WINDOWS 7 SCREEN

Before getting to the specifics of working with Windows 7, take a few seconds to familiarise yourself with the basic screen elements, including the desktop, the Start button, the taskbar, and the notification area. You will interact with these screen elements throughout your Windows 7 career, so getting familiar with them early on will help you in the long run.

### A Desktop

This is the Windows 7 "work area", meaning that it is where you work with your programs and documents.

### B Desktop Icon

An icon on the desktop represents a program, a Windows 7 feature, or a document. Programs you install often add an icon on the desktop.

### C Mouse Pointer

When you move your mouse, this pointer moves along with it.

### D Time and Date

This is the current time and date on your computer. To see the full date, position the mouse ⬚ over the time. To change the date or time, click the time.

### E Notification Area

This area displays small icons that notify you about things that are happening on your computer. For example, you see notifications if your printer runs out of paper or if an update to Windows 7 is available over the Internet.

### F Taskbar

The programs you have open appear in the taskbar. You use this area to switch between programs if you have more than one running at a time.

### G Taskbar Icons

You use these icons to launch some Windows 7 features with just a mouse click.

### H Start Button

You use this button to start programs and launch many of Windows 7's features.

# USING A MOUSE WITH WINDOWS 7

Windows 7 was built with the mouse in mind, so it pays to learn the basic mouse techniques early on because you will use them for as long as you use Windows. These techniques include clicking the mouse, double-clicking, right-clicking, and clicking-and-dragging.

If you have never used a mouse before, remember to keep all your movements slow and deliberate, and practice the techniques in this section as much as you can.

## Click the Mouse

**1** Position the mouse ⯮ over the object you want to work with.

**2** Click the left mouse button.

> **A** *Windows 7 selects the object or performs some operation in response to the click (such as displaying the Start menu).*

## Double-click the Mouse

**1** Position the mouse ⯮ over the object you want to work with.

**2** Click the left mouse button twice in quick succession.

Windows 7 usually performs some operation in response to the double-click action (such as displaying the Recycle Bin window).

## Right-click the Mouse

 Position the mouse ⤢ over the object you want to work with.

**2** Click the right mouse button.

Windows 7 displays a shortcut menu.

**Note:** *The contents of the shortcut menu depend on the object you right-clicked.*

## Click and Drag the Mouse

**1** Position the mouse ⤢ over the object you want to work with.

**2** Click and hold the left mouse button.

**3** Move the mouse to drag the selected object.

In most cases, the object moves along with the mouse ⤢.

**4** Release the mouse button when the selected object is repositioned.

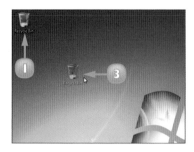

 **If you are left handed, click Start, Control Panel, Hardware and Sound, Mouse to open the Mouse Properties dialog box. Click the Buttons tab. Click Switch primary and secondary buttons (☐ changes to ☑).**

**STOP** **If your double-clicking does not work, open the Mouse Properties dialog box and click the Buttons tab. In the Double-click Speed group, click and drag the slider towards Slow.**

# GET HELP

You can find out more about Windows 7, learn how to perform a task, or troubleshoot problems by accessing the Windows 7 Help and Support system.

Most of the Windows 7 Help and Support system is arranged into categories, such as "Security and privacy" and "Files, folders, and libraries". Each category offers a number of subcategories to help you find the specific area you are looking for. Within each category and subcategory, you see a collection of related topics and these topics provide the instructions or information.

**①** Click **Start**.

The Start menu appears.

**②** Click **Help and Support**.

The Windows Help and Support window appears.

**③** Click the **Browse Help** button (🗔).

The Table of Contents appears.

**④** Click a category.

A list of Help topics appears for the category you selected.

B A list of subcategories appears for the category you selected.

5 Click a topic.

The item you selected appears in the Windows Help and Support Center window.

**Note:** *If the topic you want is part of a subcategory, click the subcategory to display the list of topics it contains and then click the topic.*

6 Read the article.

**Note:** *To return to a previous Windows Help and Support Center screen, click the* **Back** *button (⬅) until you get to the screen you want.*

 **You can access Help in a specific program by clicking Help on the menu, by pressing ⌨ or by clicking the Help button (⍰).**

# ACTIVATE YOUR COPY OF WINDOWS 7

To avoid piracy, Microsoft requires that each copy of Windows 7 be activated. Otherwise, your copy of Windows 7 will refuse to run after the activation period has expired. Activating Windows 7 means that Microsoft uses an Internet connection to confirm that your copy of Windows 7 is genuine and has not also been installed on another computer.

This section assumes that Windows 7 has not yet prompted you to start the activation. If you see an icon in the notification area with the message "Activate Windows now", click that message and then skip to Step 5.

1 Click **Start**.

The Start menu appears.

2 Right-click **Computer**.

3 Click **Properties**.

The System window appears.

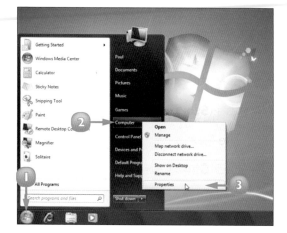

**Note:** If the System window shows the Ask for Genuine Microsoft Software, then you do not need to perform the rest of the steps in this section. Click the **Close** button () to close the System window.

4 Click the **Activate Windows now** link.

The Windows Activation dialog box appears.

5 Click **Activate Windows online now** and wait for confirmation.

6 Click **Close**.

✓ *If you do not have Internet access, in Step 5, click Show me other ways to activate. Select Use my modem to connect directly to the activation service or Use the automated phone system.*

🛑 *Activation associates your copy of the program with your computer. If the computer breaks down, Microsoft should allow you to activate Windows 7 on another computer.*

# SHUT DOWN WINDOWS 7

When you complete your work for the day, you should shut down Windows 7. However, do not just shut off your computer's power. Follow the proper steps to avoid damaging files on your system.

Shutting off the computer's power without properly exiting Windows 7 can cause two problems. First, if you have unsaved changes in some open documents, you may lose those changes. Second, you could damage one or more Windows 7 system files, which could make your system unstable.

1 Shut down all your running programs.

**Note:** *Be sure to save your work as you close your programs.*

2 Click **Start**.

The Start menu appears.

3 Click **Shut Down**.

Windows 7 shuts down and turns off your computer.

4 If you want Windows 7 to automatically reopen all the programs and documents currently on your screen, click the power button arrow () and then click **Sleep**, instead.

 *If your computer is running slow or acting funny, a restart can solve the problem. Save your work and shut down all your running programs. Click Start, click the power button arrow (▶) and click Restart. Windows 7 shuts down and your computer restarts.*

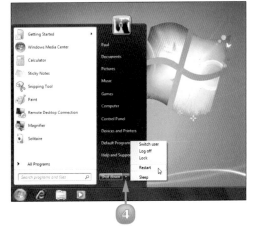

# CONTENTS

# LAUNCHING AND WORKING WITH PROGRAMS

On its own, Windows 7 does not do very much. To do something useful with your computer, you need to work with a program. At first, that will probably mean a program that comes with Windows 7, which offers a number of useful programs.

However, you can also work with any program that you install yourself, and this chapter shows you how to install programs. You also learn how to launch programs, understand program windows, and work with program pull-down menus, toolbars, dialog boxes, scrollbars, and jump lists.

# INSTALL A PROGRAM

If Windows 7 does not come with a program that you need, you can obtain the program yourself, either from a computer store or via an Internet download. You can then install the program on your computer.

How you start the installation process depends on what format the program comes in. If you purchased the program from a store, then the program comes on a CD or DVD disc, and you use that disc to install the program. If you downloaded the program from the Internet, the program comes in the downloaded file, and you use that file to install the program.

## Install from a CD or DVD

1. Insert the program's disc into your computer's CD or DVD drive.

   The AutoPlay dialog box appears.

2. Click **Run *file***, where *file* is the name of the installation program (usually SETUP.EXE).

3. Follow the installation instructions the program provides.

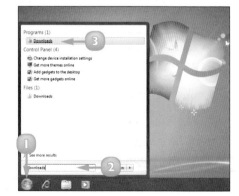

## Install from a Downloaded File

1. Click **Start**.

2. Type **downloads**.

3. Click **Downloads**.

**Note:** *If you saved the file into another folder, use Windows Explorer to find it (see the "View Your Files" section in Chapter 6).*

   The Downloads folder appears.

4. Double-click the file.

   The software's installation program begins.

5. Follow the installation instructions the program provides.

 **Many programs need a product key or serial number. A sticker is attached to the CD case or the back of the box; the key for a downloaded program appears on the download screen or e-mail receipt.**

# CHANGE OR REPAIR A PROGRAM INSTALLATION

When you install a program, you can choose the "custom" installation option to install only some of the program's components. If you decide later to install more components or remove installed components, you can rerun the installation program to make these changes.

If an installed program does not start or behaves erratically, it may have one or more missing or corrupt files. Many programs come with a repair option that can fix such problems.

**1** Click **Start**.

**2** Click **Control Panel**.

The Control Panel window appears.

**3** Click **Uninstall a program**.

The Programs and Features window appears.

**A** *Windows 7 displays a list of the programs installed on your computer.*

**4** Click the program you want to work with.

**5** Click **Change**.

**Note:** *For some programs, you click* ***Uninstall/Change****. If you want to repair the program, click* ***Repair****.*

**6** Follow the installation instructions the program provides.

 **In almost all cases, repairing a program simply copies the program's original files to your hard disk. You should back up your data (see Chapter 12) before repairing any program because you could lose data that you have created.**

# START A PROGRAM

To work with any program, you must first tell Windows 7 what program you want to run. You normally do this by selecting the program via the Windows 7 Start menu, which contains a list of the programs you use most often, as well as various submenus that contain icons for all the programs installed on your computer. In Windows 7, you can also use the taskbar to start some programs.

Whichever method you use, Windows 7 then launches the program and displays it on the desktop.

① Click **Start**.

If the program you want to use has a taskbar button, you can click the button to launch the program.

② Click **All Programs**.

**Note:** When you click **All Programs**, the command name changes to Back.

③ If your program icon is in a submenu, click the submenu.

④ Click the icon for the program you want to launch.

Ⓐ The program appears on the desktop.

Ⓑ Windows 7 adds a button for the program to the taskbar.

**Note:** After you have used a program a few times, it may appear on the main Start menu. If so, you can launch the program by clicking its Start menu icon.

# UNDERSTANDING PROGRAM WINDOWS

When you start a program, it appears on the Windows 7 desktop in its own window. You work with a program by manipulating the various features of its window. These features include the title bar, menu bar, toolbar, and three buttons: Minimize, Maximize, and Close.

### A System Menu Icon

Clicking this icon or pressing  + **Spacebar** displays a menu that enables you to work with program windows via the keyboard.

### B Title Bar

The title bar displays the name of the program. In some programs, the title bar also displays the name of the open document. You can also use the title bar to move the window.

### C Menu Bar

The menu bar contains the pull-down menus for Windows 7 and most Windows 7 software. In some programs, you must press **Alt** to see the menu bar.

### D Toolbar

These buttons offer easy access to common program commands and features. Some buttons are commands and some have lists from which you can make a choice.

### E Minimize Button

You click the Minimize button () to remove the window from the desktop and display only the window's taskbar button. The window is still open, but not active.

### F Maximize Button

To enlarge the window from the taskbar or so that it takes up the entire desktop, you click the Maximize button (🔲).

### G Close Button

When you click the Close button (❎), the program shuts down.

# USE PULL-DOWN MENUS

When you are ready to work with a program, Windows 7 offers a number of different methods, but the pull-down menus are the most common. You use pull-down menus to access the program's commands and features.

There are two types of items in most pull-down menus: commands that execute some action in the program, or features that you turn on and off.

You access all pull-down menus via the menu bar, and most programs display the menu bar by default. However, if you do not see the menu bar, you can often display it by pressing the Alt key.

## Run Commands

1 Click the name of the menu you want to display.

The program displays the menu.

You can also display a menu by pressing and holding Alt and pressing the underlined letter in the menu name.

2 Click the command you want to run.

The program runs the command.

If a submenu appears, click the command in the submenu.

## Turn Features On and Off

1 Click the name of the menu you want to display.

The program displays the menu.

2 Click a menu item.

Toggle features are either turned on (indicated by ☑) or off (no check mark appears).

The active option feature is indicated by ⦿.

# USE TOOLBARS

You can use a program's toolbars to access commands faster than using the pull-down menus. In most cases, a toolbar is a collection of buttons, lists, or other controls that often give you one-click access to the program's most common features.

Most programs come with one or more toolbars, although in some programs you must first display the toolbar you need. If there is a toolbar that you never use, you can hide it to give yourself more room in the program window.

## Execute Commands

① Click the toolbar button that represents the command or list.

**Note:** *If the toolbar button remains "pressed" after you click it, the button toggles a feature on and off and the feature is now on. To turn the feature off, click the button to "unpress" it.*

The program executes the command or, as shown here, drops down the list.

② If a list appears, click the list item for the command.

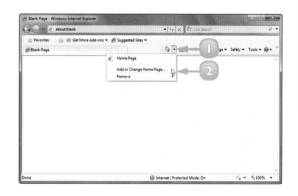

## Display and Hide Toolbars

① Click **View**.

② Click **Toolbars**.

③ Click a toolbar.

If the toolbar is currently displayed (indicated by ☑ in the View menu), the program hides the toolbar. If the toolbar is currently hidden, the program displays the toolbar.

# USE DIALOG BOXES

You use dialog boxes to control how a program works. Dialog boxes appear frequently, so you need to know how to use them to get the most out of any program.

For example, when you print a document, you usually see the Print dialog box, which includes several controls that enable you to control the print job. You might see a list of the available printers, radio buttons that enable you to specify how much of the document you want to print, and a spin button that enables you to specify the number of copies you want printed.

## Use a Text Box

**①** Click inside the text box.

A blinking, vertical bar (called a *cursor* or an *insertion point*) appears inside the text box.

Use **Backspace** or **Del** to delete any existing characters.

Type your text.

## Enter a Value with a Spin Button

**①** Click the top arrow on the spin button (⬆) to increase the value.

**②** Click the bottom arrow on the spin button (⬇) to decrease the value.

You can also type a value in the text box.

## Select a List Box Item

 If necessary, click the down arrow (☐) to scroll down the list and bring the item you want to select into view.

Click the up arrow (☐) to scroll back up through the list.

**Note:** *See the "Using Scrollbars" section to learn how to use scrollbars.*

 Click the item.

## Select an Item Using a Combo Box

 Click the item in the list box to select it.

② You can also type the item name in the text box.

## Select an Item From a Drop-Down List Box

 Click the drop-down arrow (☐).

The list appears.

④ Click the item in the list that you want to select.

✓ **These keyboard shortcuts make dialog boxes easier to work with.**

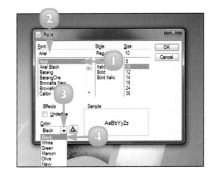

| Enter | Selects the default command button (which is indicated with a highlight around it). |
|---|---|
| Esc | Cancels the dialog box (which is the same as clicking Cancel). |
| Alt +letter | Selects the control that has the letter underlined. |
| Tab | Moves forward through the dialog box controls. |
| Shift + Tab | Moves backward through the dialog box controls. |
| ↑ and ↓ | Moves up and down within the current option button group. |
| Alt + ↓ | Drops down the selected combo box or drop-down list box. |

# WORK WITH PROGRAM WINDOWS

You need to know how to work with program windows so that you can keep your desktop neat and your programs easier to find.

For example, you can minimise a window to clear it from the desktop and you can maximise a window to give yourself more room to work within the window. You should also know how to *restore* a window. This means that you return the window to its original size and location after you have minimised or maximised it. You also need to know how to close a window that you no longer need.

24

## Minimise a Window

1 Click the **Minimize** button (▬).

> **A** *The window disappears from the screen, but its taskbar button remains visible.*

## Maximise a Window

2 Click the **Maximize** button (▢).

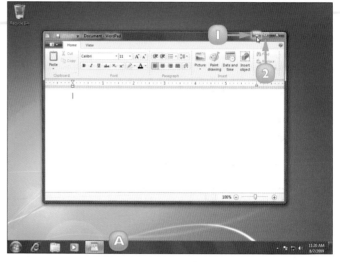

The window enlarges to fill the entire desktop.

**Note:** *You can also maximise a window by double-clicking its title bar or by dragging its title bar to the top of the screen.*

 **To see your desktop, position the mouse ☇ over the Show desktop bar on the right edge of the taskbar.**

**To minimise all your open windows, click the Show desktop bar or right-click the taskbar and then click Show the desktop.**

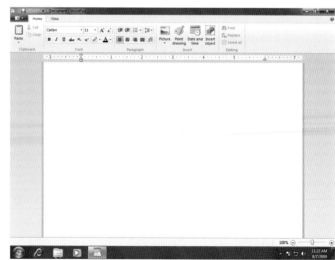

## Restore a Window

 If the window is maximised, click the **Restore** button ().

If the window is minimised, click its taskbar button.

The window returns to its previous size and location.

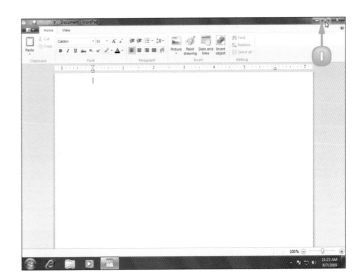

## Close a Window

 Click the **Close** button (![x]).

The window disappears from the screen.

If the window has a taskbar button, the button disappears from the taskbar.

**Note:** *If the window contains a document, the program may ask if you want to save any changes you made in the document before closing.*

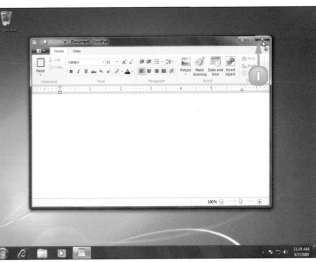

☑ **To maximise a minimised window, right-click the window's taskbar button. In the menu, click Maximize.**

☑ **Press Alt + Spacebar to display the system menu for a window. Use ⬆ and ⬇ to highlight the command you want and then press Enter.**

continued ➡

25

If you have information on the desktop or in a window that you want to see, but another window is covering some or all of that information, you can move the other window out of the way.

If after moving the window you find that it still covers up part of the other item, you can also resize the window.

Similarly, if your windows overlap each other, making it hard to read what is in other windows, you can move the windows around or resize them.

## Change the Window Size

 Position the mouse ▷ over the window border that you want to move.

 The ▷ changes to a two-headed arrow (↕).

**Note:** *If the pointer does not change, it means the window cannot be resized.*

② Click and drag the ↕ to make the window larger or smaller.

Windows 7 moves the border along with the ↕.

③ Release the mouse button.

Windows 7 resizes the window.

**Note:** *To resize two borders at once, click and drag the corner of the window that joins them.*

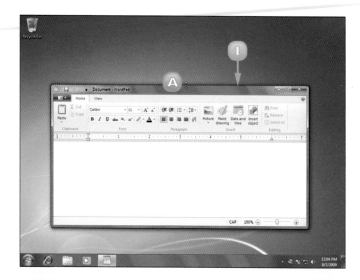

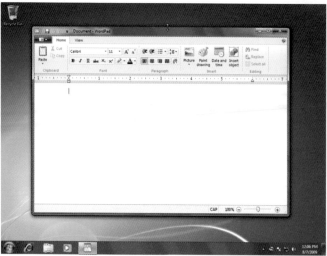

## Move a Window

**①** Position the mouse ⌨ over an empty section of the window's title bar.

**②** Click and drag the mouse ⌨ in the direction you want the window to move.

Windows 7 moves the window along with the mouse ⌨.

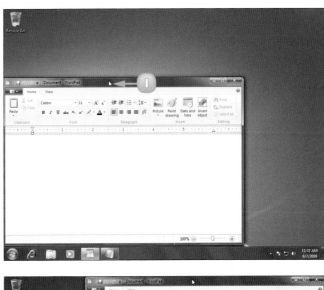

**③** Release the mouse button.

Windows 7 moves the window.

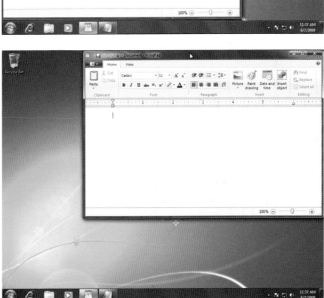

✓ *Press* **Alt**+**Spacebar** *to display the system menu. If you choose* **Move** *or* **Size**, *use the arrow keys to move or size the window, and then press* **Enter**. *Press* **Ctrl**+**F4** *to close a program window.*

✓ *To stop windows overlapping, right-click an empty section of the taskbar and then click* **Show windows side by side**. *Windows 7 divides the desktop to give each window an equal amount of space.*

✓ *To stack windows, right-click an empty section of the taskbar and then click* **Show windows stacked**. *Windows 7 arranges the windows in a tidy diagonal pattern from the top left corner of the desktop.*

# USE SCROLLBARS

If the entire content of a document is too long to fit inside a window, you can see the rest of the document by using the window's vertical scrollbar to move the content up and down.

In some scenarios, the content may be too wide to fit inside a window. In such cases, you can see the rest of the document by using the window's horizontal scrollbar to move the content left and right.

Scrollbars also appear in many list boxes, so knowing how to work with scrollbars also helps you use dialog boxes.

## Scroll Up or Down in a Window

1 Click and drag the vertical scroll box down or up to scroll through a window.

A *You can also click the up arrow (▲) or down arrow (▲).*

B *The text scrolls down or up.*

## Scroll Right or Left in a Window

 Click and drag the horizontal scroll box.

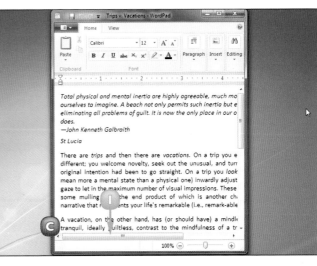

C You can also click the right arrow (▶) or the left arrow (◀).

D *The text scrolls left or right.*

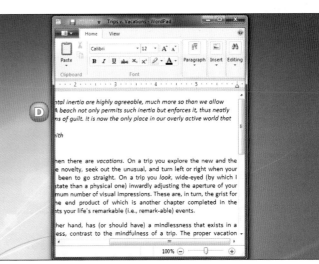

✓ *If your mouse has a wheel, you can use it for scrolling up or down in a document. Move the wheel backward, toward your arm, and the document scrolls down; move the wheel forward, toward your computer, and the document scrolls up.*

# SWITCH BETWEEN PROGRAMS

With Windows 7, you can run two or more programs at the same time, a technique called *multitasking*. For example, you could have your word processor, your e-mail program, and your Web browser running at the same time. However many programs you are currently multitasking, you need to know how to switch from one to another.

You can switch from one program to another by using either the taskbar or the keyboard.

## Switch Programs Using the Taskbar

**1** Click the taskbar button of the program to which you want to switch.

**Note:** *A program does not have to be minimised to the taskbar for you to use the program's taskbar button.*

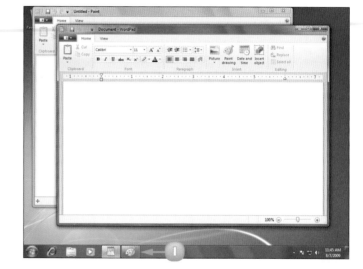

**A** *Windows 7 brings the program's window to the foreground.*

**Note:** *You can also switch to another window by clicking the window, even if it is in the background.*

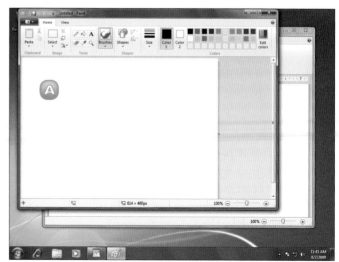

## Switch Programs Using the Keyboard

1. Press and hold **Alt** and press **Tab**.

   Windows 7 displays thumbnail versions of the open windows and the desktop.

2. Press **Tab** until the window in which you want to work is selected.

3. Release **Alt**.

4. Windows 7 brings the program's window to the foreground.

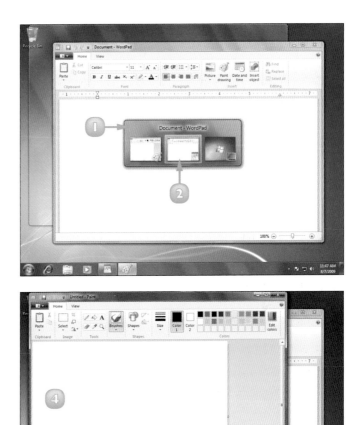

 *Position the mouse ⃟ over a program's taskbar button to see a thumbnail of the program window before switching to it.*

# TAKE ADVANTAGE OF PROGRAM JUMP LISTS

You can use the new jump list feature in Windows 7 to open files or run program tasks. A *jump list* is a list associated with each program that supports this feature. Most jump lists consist of items you most recently used in the program, but some jump lists also include common program tasks.

The recent items you see on a program's jump list are called *destinations*, and they can be files, folders, Web sites, or whatever type of data the program supports.

## Open a Destination

① Right-click the program's taskbar icon.

② Click the destination.

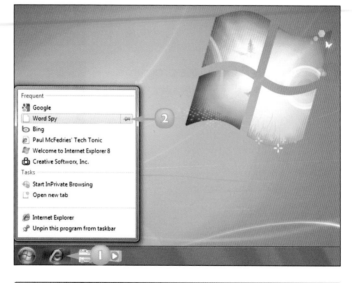

Windows 7 launches the program if it is not already running and opens the destination.

## Run a Task

 Right-click the program's taskbar icon.

 Click the task.

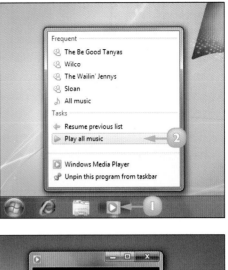

Windows 7 launches the program if it is not already running and runs the task.

You can pin a destination to the jump list, so that it always appears. If the destination is already on the jump list, right-click it and click **Pin to this list.**

To remove or unpin a destination from a jump list, right-click the destination and then click **Remove from this list** or **Unpin from this list.**

# UNINSTALL A PROGRAM

When you plan to no longer use a program, you should uninstall it from your computer. Uninstalling a program means that you delete all of the program's files from your computer and remove the program's icons from the Start menu, desktop, and taskbar. Fortunately, either the program itself or Windows 7 takes care of all these uninstall details automatically, so you only need to start the process.

Removing unused programs frees up disk space and makes your All Programs menu easier to navigate.

34

① Click **Start**.

② Click **Control Panel**.

The Control Panel window appears.

③ Click **Uninstall a program**.

The Installed Programs window appears.

④ Click the program you want to uninstall.

⑤ Click **Uninstall** (or **Uninstall/ Change**).

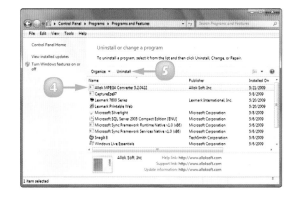

In most cases, the program asks you to confirm that you want to uninstall it.

⑥ Click **Yes**.

The program's uninstall procedure begins. Follow the instructions on the screen, which vary from program to program.

✓ *Many programs come with an uninstall command. Click* **Start, All Programs** *and the program name. Click the command that includes the word* **Uninstall** *to begin the uninstall procedure.*

# CONTENTS

# 3

## CREATING AND EDITING DOCUMENTS

To get productive with Windows 7, you need to know how to work with documents. In this chapter, you begin by learning what documents are and what types of documents you can create. From there, you learn how to create your own documents and how to save your work. You also get the details on opening documents and you learn basic editing techniques, such as deleting characters, selecting text, and copying and moving text. You also learn how to change the font, find and replace text, and print documents.

# UNDERSTANDING DOCUMENTS

Although your computer comes with thousands of files, only a few of them can be considered documents. That is because a document is a file that you create yourself or that you can open and edit yourself.

Most documents consist of text, but you can also create documents that are pictures. The four examples shown here are the basic document types that you can create using the programs that come with Windows 7.

## Text Document

A text document is one that includes only the characters that you see on your keyboard, plus a few others. A text document contains no special formatting, such as coloured text or bold formatting, although you can change the font. In Windows 7, you normally use the Notepad program to create text documents (although you can also use WordPad).

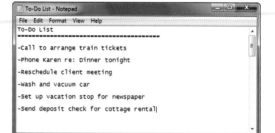

## Word Processing Document

A word processing document contains text and other symbols, but you can format those characters to improve the look of the document. For example, you can change the size, colour, and typeface, and you can make words bold or italic. In Windows 7, you use the WordPad program to create word processing – or Rich Text Format – documents.

## Drawing

A drawing in this context is a digital image you create using "tools" that draw lines, boxes, polygons, special effects, and free-form shapes. In Windows 7, you use the Paint program to create drawings.

## E-mail Message

An e-mail message is a document that you send to another person via the Internet. Most e-mail messages use plain text, but some programs support formatted text, images, and other effects. In Windows 7, you can download and install the Windows Live Mail program to create and send e-mail messages (see Chapter 9).

# CREATE A DOCUMENT

When you are ready to create something using Windows 7, in most cases you begin by opening the appropriate program – such as Windows Live Mail, if you want to create an e-mail message – and then using the program to create a new document to hold your work.

Many Windows 7 programs (such as WordPad and Paint) create a new document for you automatically when you begin the program. However, you can also create a new document any time you need one.

 **Ⓐ** *Start the program you want to work with.*

**❶** Click **File**.

**❷** Click **New**.

**Ⓑ** *If the program supports more than one type of file, the program asks which type you want to create.*

**Note:** *Some programs display a dialog box with a list of document types.*

**❸** Click the document type you want.

The program creates the new document.

**Note:** *In some programs you can also create a document by clicking the **New Document** toolbar button (). In most programs, you can also press Ctrl+N to create a new document.*

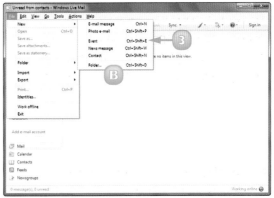

# SAVE A DOCUMENT

After you create a document and make any changes to it, you can save the document to preserve your work.

Saving your work is important because when you work on a document, Windows 7 stores the changes in your computer's memory, which is erased each time you shut down or restart your computer. When you save a document, Windows 7 stores your changes on your computer's hard drive. Because the contents of the hard drive are preserved when you shut down or restart your computer, you do not lose your work.

**①** Click **File** (🔲).

**②** Click **Save**.

**Note:** *If you have saved the document previously, your changes are now preserved. You do not need to follow the rest of the steps in this section.*

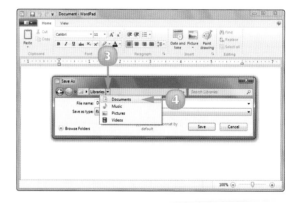

If this is a new document that you have never saved before, the Save As dialog box appears.

**③** Click here to see a list of your folders.

**④** Click **Documents**.

**Note:** *In most programs, the Documents folder is selected automatically when you save a document.*

 **In most programs, you can also press** Ctrl+S **or click the Save button (🔲).**

Windows 7 opens the
Documents folder.

⑤ Click in the File Name text box
and type the name you want to
use for the document.

**Note:** *The name you type can be up to 255
characters long, but it cannot include the
following characters: < > , ? : " \ *.*

⑥ Click **Save**.

Ⓐ *The file name you typed
appears in the program's
title bar.*

**WordPad can create word
processing documents and
text documents but Notepad
supports only text documents.
If a program supports multiple
document types, the Save As
dialog box includes a drop-
down list named Save As Type
(or something similar).**

# OPEN A DOCUMENT

To work with a document that you have saved in the past, you need to open the document in the program that you used to create it.

When you save a document, Windows 7 stores the document contents in a file on your hard drive. Opening the document means that Windows 7 locates the file on the hard drive and then loads its contents into your computer's memory. This enables you to read, edit, and add to the document using the original program.

① Start the program you want to work with.

② Click **File** ().

**Note:** *If you see the document you want in the list of recently used documents on the File menu, click the name to open it and skip the rest of the steps in this section.*

③ Click **Open**.

The Open dialog box appears.

④ Double-click **Documents**.

**Note:** *In most programs, the Documents folder is selected automatically when you open a document.*

Ⓐ *If you want to open the document from some other folder, click here, click your user name, and then double-click the folder.*

Windows 7 opens the Documents folder.

**In most programs, you can also press** Ctrl+O **or click the Open button (**▣**).**

42

Click the document name.

 Click **Open**.

The document appears in the program window.

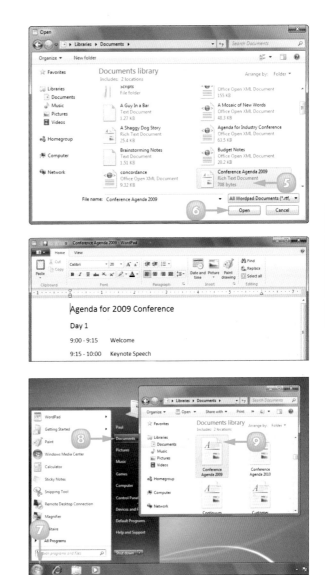

You do not always need to open a program before opening a document.

 Click **Start**.

 Click **Documents**.

The Documents library appears.

 Double-click the document.

Windows 7 starts the program in which you created the document and then opens the document.

# EDIT DOCUMENT TEXT

When you work with a character-based file, such as a text document, a word processing document, or an e-mail message, you need to know the basic techniques for editing the document text.

The most fundamental editing technique involves deleting existing characters that you no longer need or that you typed accidentally or in error. However, you also need to know how to select text, which then enables you to copy or move that text.

## Delete Characters

1 Click immediately to the left of the first character you want to delete.

The cursor appears before the character.

2 Press **Del** until you have deleted all the characters you want.

**Note:** *An alternative method is to click immediately to the right of the last character you want to delete and then press* **Backspace** *until you have deleted all the characters you want.*

**Note:** *If you make a mistake, immediately press* **Ctrl** + **Z** *or click the* **Undo** *button (*■*). Alternatively, click* **Edit** *and then click* **Undo***.*

44

## Select Text for Editing

① Click and drag across the text you want to select.

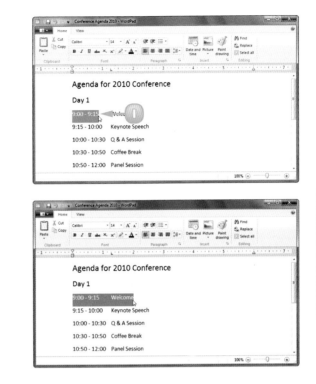

② Release the mouse button.

The program highlights the selected text.

**Here are some useful shortcut methods for selecting text in WordPad:**

✓ **Click in the white space to the left of a line to select the line.**

✓ **Double-click a word to select it.**

✓ **Triple-click inside a paragraph to select it.**

✓ **Press Ctrl + A to select the entire document.**

✓ **For a long selection, click to the left of the first character you want to select, scroll to the end of the selection using the scroll bar, press and hold Shift, and then click to the right of the last character you want to select.**

continued ➡

Once you select some text, the program treats the selection as though it was a single object. This means that you can work with all of the selected characters together, which is much faster than working with one character at a time.

For example, if you need to delete a large section of text, it is much faster to select the text first and then delete it all at once. You can also copy or move the selected text to a different location within the document.

## Copy Text

**1** Select the text you want to copy.

**2** Click **Copy** (▣).

**Note:** *In most programs, you can also press* **Ctrl** + **C** *or click the* **Edit** *menu and then click* **Copy***.*

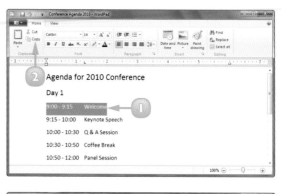

**3** Click inside the document at the position where you want the copy of the text to appear.

The cursor appears in the position you clicked.

**4** Click **Paste** (▢).

**Note:** *In most programs, you can also press* **Ctrl** + **V** *or click the* **Edit** *menu and then click* **Paste***.*

The program inserts a copy of the selected text at the cursor position.

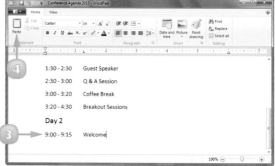

## Move Text

1. Select the text you want to move.
2. Click **Cut** (✂).

   The program removes the text from the document.

**Note:** *In most programs, you can also press* Ctrl + X *or click the* ***Edit*** *menu and then click* ***Cut****.*

3. Click inside the document at the position where you want to move the text.

   The cursor appears at the position you clicked.

4. Click **Paste** (📋).

   The program inserts the text at the cursor position.

**Note:** *In most programs, you can also press* Ctrl + V *or click the* ***Edit*** *menu and then click* ***Paste****.*

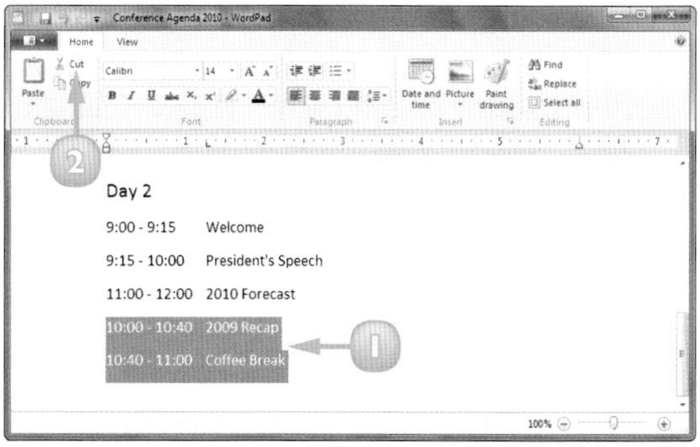


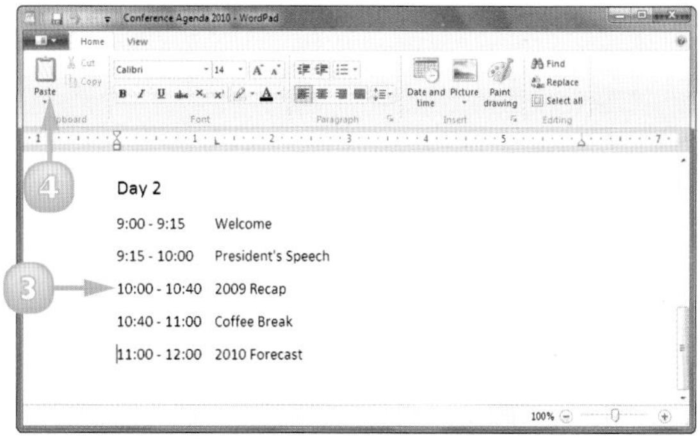


***Select the text you want to move or copy with your mouse and position the mouse ⇖ over the selection. To move it, click and drag the text to the new position within the document. To copy it, press and hold Ctrl, and then click and drag the text to the desired position.***

# CHANGE THE TEXT FONT

When you work in a word processing document, you can add visual appeal by changing the font formatting of some or all of the text.

The font formatting determines how the characters appear in the document. For example, one common font attribute is the typeface, which determines the overall look of each character. You can also change the font style – which determines whether the text appears as bold or italic – and the font size. Most programs also offer several special effects, such as underline or colours.

 Select the text you want to format.

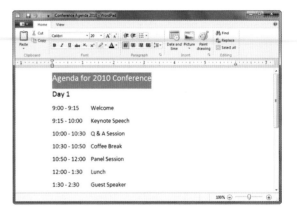

② Click the **Home** tab.

Ⓐ *WordPad displays the font options.*

**Note:** *In many other programs, you display the font options by clicking* **Format** *in the menu bar and then clicking the* **Font** *command.*

③ Click ⊡ to see the list of fonts.

④ In the Font list, click the typeface you want.

⑤ In the Size list, click the type size you want.

⑥ For bold text, click **Bold** (B).

⑦ For italics, click *Italic* (I).

⑧ For underlining, click **Underline** (U).

⑨ In the Font colour list, click ⊡ and then click a colour.

The program applies the font formatting to the selected text.

*These shortcuts work in most programs: for bold, press Ctrl + B; for italics, press Ctrl + I; for underline, press Ctrl + U.*

# FIND TEXT

In large documents, when you need to find a specific word or phrase, you can save a lot of time by using the program's Find feature, which searches the entire document in the blink of an eye.

Most programs that work with text — including Windows 7's WordPad and Notepad programs — have the Find feature. You can also work with the Find feature in programs such as Internet Explorer and Windows Live Mail.

1  Click **Find** ().

**Note:** *In many programs, you run the Find command by clicking **Edit** in the menu bar and then clicking the **Find** command or by pressing* Ctrl *+* F *.*

The Find dialog box appears.

2  Click in the Find What text box and type the text you want to find.

3  Click **Find Next**.

**A** The program selects the next instance of the search text.

**Note:** *If the search text does not exist in the document, the program usually displays a dialog box to let you know.*

**4** If the selected instance is not the one you want, click **Find Next** until the program finds the correct instance.

**5** Click the **Close** button (☒) to close the Find dialog box.

The program leaves the found text selected.

To avoid matching small words, such as "the", in words such as "theme" and "bother", click **Match whole word only** (☐ changes to ☑) in the Find dialog box.

To avoid matching the name "Bill" with the word "bill", click **Match case** (☐ changes to ☑) in the Find dialog box.

# REPLACE TEXT

Do you need to replace a word or part of a word with some other text? Normally you would open the document and then edit the text directly. However, if you have several instances to replace, you can save time and do a more accurate job if you let the program's Replace feature make the changes for you.

Most programs that work with text – including Windows 7's WordPad and Notepad programs – have the Replace feature.

① Click **Replace** (🔄).

**Note:** *In many programs, you run the Find command by clicking **Edit** in the menu bar and then clicking the **Replace** command or by pressing* Ctrl + H.

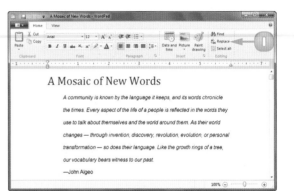

The Replace dialog box appears.

② In the Find What text box, enter the text you want to find.

③ Click in the Replace With text box and type the text you want to use as the replacement.

④ Click **Find Next**.

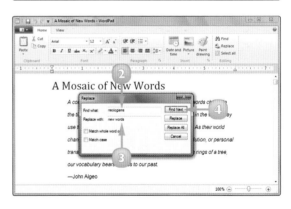

**A** The program selects the next instance of the search text.

**Note:** If the search text does not exist in the document, the program displays a dialog box to let you know.

**5** If the selected instance is not the one you want, click **Find Next** until the program finds the correct instance.

**6** Click **Replace**.

**B** The program replaces the selected text with the replacement text.

**C** The program selects the next instance of the search text.

**7** Repeat Steps **5** and **6** until you have replaced all of the instances you want to replace.

**8** Click the **Close** button (❌) to close the Replace dialog box.

**To replace every instance of the search text with the replacement text, click Replace All in the Replace dialog box. You should exercise some caution with this feature because it may make some replacements that you did not intend.**

# PRINT A DOCUMENT

When you need a hard copy of your document, either for your files or to distribute to someone else, you can get a paper copy by sending the document to your printer. If you happen to have more than one printer, you can specify which device you prefer to use for the document.

All programs enable you to specify in advance how many copies you want to print. In most cases, you can also tell the program to print only part of the document, if that is all you need.

① Turn on your printer.

② Open the document you want to print.

③ Click **File** ().

④ Click **Print**.

**Note:** *In many programs, you can select the* **Print** *command by pressing* `Ctrl` + `P` *or by clicking the* **Print** *button (* ◄ *).*

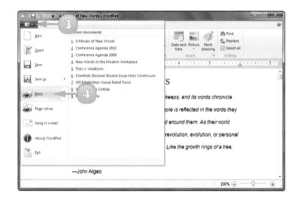

The Print dialog box appears.

**Note:** *The layout of the Print dialog box varies from program to program. The WordPad version shown here is a typical example.*

⑤ If you have more than one printer, click the printer you want to use.

⑥ Use the **Number of copies** (⊞) to specify the number of copies to print.

⑦ Click **Print**.

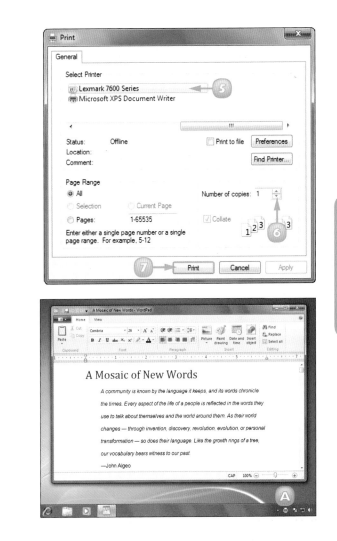

Ⓐ Windows 7 prints the document. The print icon (🖨) appears in the taskbar's notification area while the document prints.

✓ **Most programs enable you to print only part of a document:**

✓ **Select the text you want to print; in the Print dialog box, click Selection (◎ changes to ◉).**

✓ **Place the cursor on the page you want to print; in the Print dialog box, click Current Page (◎ changes to ◉).**

✓ **In the Print dialog box, click Pages (◎ changes to ◉). In the text box, type the first page number, a dash (-), and the last page number (for example, 1-5).**

# CONTENTS

# 4

## WORKING WITH IMAGES

Whether you load your images from a device, download them from the Internet, or draw them yourself, Windows 7 comes with a number of useful tools for working with those images. For example, you can use the Pictures library to see a preview of an image and to open an image for viewing. You can also use Windows 7 to scan a photo or other image from a scanner, and you can import photos that you have taken with a digital camera. You can also make repairs to an image and print hard copies of your photos.

# OPEN THE PICTURES LIBRARY

Before you can work with your images, you need to view them on your computer. You do that by opening Windows 7's Pictures library, which is a special folder designed specifically for storing images.

As you see later in this chapter, you can use the Pictures library to preview an image and open an image file. Also, when you import an image using a scanner or digital camera, Windows 7 usually stores the resulting files in the Pictures library.

 Click **Start**.

② Click **Pictures**.

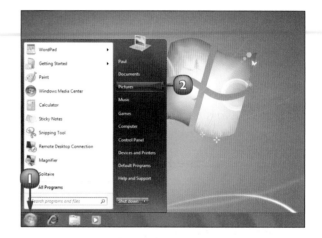

The Pictures library appears.

# PREVIEW AN IMAGE

You can preview any saved image file using either the Details pane or the Preview pane in the Pictures library. The Details pane also displays details about the file, such as the file type, dimensions, and size. The Preview pane shows a larger preview of the image. You can also use the Preview pane to preview images stored in *subfolders* – folders stored within the main Pictures library.

① Click the image file you want to preview.

Ⓐ *The Details pane shows a small preview of the image.*

Ⓑ *Details about the image file appear here.*

② Click **Show the Preview Pane** (▣).

Windows 7 opens the Preview pane and displays a larger preview of the image.

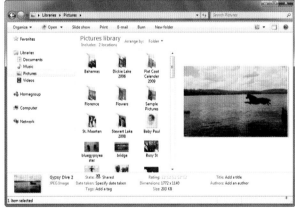

# VIEW YOUR IMAGES

If you want to look at several images, you can use Windows Photo Viewer to navigate backwards and forwards through the images in the Pictures library.

You can also view the images in your Pictures library using Windows Live Photo Gallery, if you have that program installed on your computer. See Chapter 9 to learn how to install Windows Live Photo Gallery. You can use either program to zoom in and out of an image and to run an image slide show.

## View Images using Windows Photo Viewer

1 Click the image.

2 Click the **Open** ⊡.

3 Click **Windows Photo Viewer**.

The image opens in Windows Photo Viewer.

4 To get a closer look at the image, click the magnifying glass and then click and drag the slider up.

5 To view the next image in the folder, click the **Next** button ().

6 To view the previous image in the folder, click the **Previous** button (◀).

7 To start a slide show of all the images in the folder, click the **Play Slide Show** button (▢).

**Note:** To stop the slide show, press Esc.

## View Images using Windows Live Photo Gallery

 Click the image.

2 Click the **Open** ⊡.

3 Click **Windows Live Photo Gallery**.

The image opens in Windows Live Photo Gallery.

4 To see more of the image, click and drag the slider to the right.

5 To view the next image in the folder, click the **Next** button (▶).

6 To view the previous image in the folder, click the **Previous** button (◀).

7 To start a slide show of all the images in the folder, click the **Play Slide Show** button (▣).

**Note:** To stop the slide show, press Esc.

> *You can change the Picture folder's view to display large thumbnails – scaled-down versions of the actual images. Click the Views ⊡ and Extra Large Icons.*

# SCAN AN IMAGE

You can create a digital copy of a photo or other image by using a document scanner, or the scanner component of an all-in-one printer. The scanner copies the image to your computer, where you can then store it as a file on your hard drive.

There are many ways you can use a scanned image. For example, you can scan a photo to e-mail to friends or publish on a Web page. You can also scan a logo or other image to use in a document.

① Turn on your scanner or all-in-one printer and position a photo or other image on the scanner bed.

② Click **Start**.

③ Click **Devices and Printers**.

The Devices and Printers window appears.

④ Click the device you want to use to perform the scan.

⑤ Click **Start scan**.

The New Scan dialog box appears.

 Click the **Profile** ⊡ and then click **Photo**.

 Click the **Resolution** ⊟ to specify the scan resolution.

**Note:** *The higher the resolution, the sharper the image, but the larger the resulting file.*

 Click **Preview**.

A preview of the scan appears in the grey box.

 Click and drag the edges of the dashed rectangle to set the scan area.

 Click **Scan**.

Windows 7 scans the image.

The Importing Pictures and Videos dialog box appears.

 Type a word or phrase that describes the scan.

 Click **Import**.

Windows 7 imports the image to your computer.

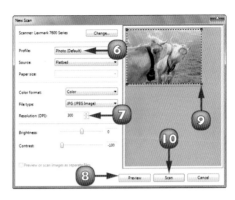

*Windows 7 stores scanned images in the Pictures library in a new folder, the name of which is the current date followed by the text you type in the Importing Pictures and Videos dialog box; for example, 2009-08-23 Flower.*

*Most scanners and all-in-one printers come with a Scan button that you can push to start a new scan. In Windows Fax and Scan, you can click New Scan. In Paint and Windows Live Photo Gallery, you can click File and then select the option to import from a camera or scanner.*

# IMPORT IMAGES FROM A DIGITAL CAMERA

If you have used your digital camera to take pictures, you can use Windows 7 to import those photos from the camera and save them on your computer. If your camera stores the photos on a memory card, you can also use a memory card reader attached to your computer to upload the digital photos from the removable drive that Windows 7 sets up.

Once you have the digital photos on your system, you can view the photos, make repairs or adjustments to the files, or print the images.

 Plug in your camera or memory storage card reader.

The AutoPlay dialog box appears.

② Click **Import Pictures and Videos using Windows**.

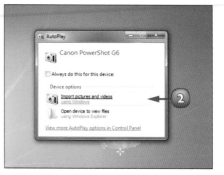

The Import Pictures and Videos dialog box appears.

③ Type a word or phrase that describes the photos.

④ Click **Import**.

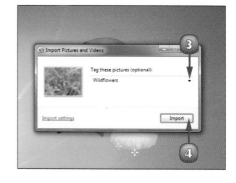

Windows 7 begins importing the digital photos.

**5** To have Windows 7 erase the photos from the camera or card, click **Erase after importing** (☐ changes to ☑).

The Imported Pictures and Videos window appears and displays the recently imported photos.

**6** When you have finished looking at your photos, click the **Close** button (☒) to close the window.

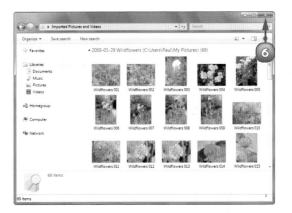

*Windows 7 stores imported digital photos in the Pictures library in a new folder, the name of which is the current date followed by the text you type in the Importing Pictures and Videos dialog box. For example, 2009-08-23 Nassau Vacation.*

# REPAIR A DIGITAL IMAGE

You can use Windows Live Photo Gallery to improve the look of digital photos and other images. Windows Live Photo Gallery includes a special Fix window that offers a number of tools for repairing various image attributes.

The Fix window enables you to adjust an image's brightness, contrast, colour temperature, tint, and saturation. You can also crop and rotate an image and fix red eye. Windows Live Photo Gallery also comes with a feature that can make many of these adjustments for you automatically. See Chapter 9 to learn how to download and install Windows Live Photo Gallery.

 Click **Start**.

 Click **All Programs**.

**Note:** When you click **All Programs**, the command name changes to Back.

③ Click **Windows Live**.

④ Click **Windows Live Photo Gallery**.

Windows Live Photo Gallery appears.

⑤ Click the image you want to repair.

⑥ Click **Fix** to open the Fix window.

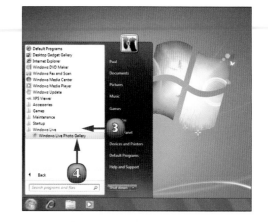

66

**7** To change the exposure, click **Adjust exposure** and then click and drag the **Brightness** and **Contrast** sliders.

**8** To change the colour, click **Adjust color** and then click and drag the **Color temperature**, **Tint**, and **Saturation** sliders.

**A** *If you are not sure how to use these tools, click **Auto adjust** to have Photo Gallery make the adjustments for you.*

**9** To remove red eye from a photo, click **Fix red eye**.

**10** To crop the picture, click **Crop photo**.

**11** Click the **Proportion** ⊡ and choose a dimension.

**Note:** *Click **Original** to keep the same relative height and width; click **Custom** to crop to any height and width.*

**12** Click and drag the handles to set the new size.

**13** Click **Apply**.

**14** When you are done, click **Back to gallery**.

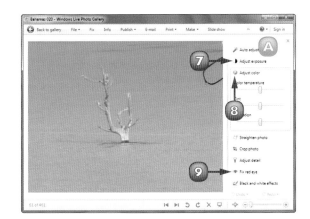

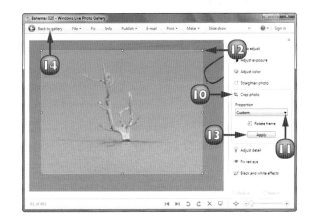

 *When you take a vertical shot with your digital camera, the photo appears sideways when you download it to your computer. In the Fix window, click 🔄 to rotate the image counterclockwise; click 🔃 to rotate the image clockwise.*

*Windows Live Photo Gallery keeps a backup copy of the original image. If you do not like the repairs you made, you can undo your changes: click the image and then click Fix, Revert and Revert to Original (or press Ctrl + R).*

# PRINT AN IMAGE

You can print an image from the Pictures library, or from any subfolder in the Pictures library. When you activate the Print task, the Print Pictures dialog box appears. You can use this dialog box to choose a printer, the paper size, the printout quality, and a layout, and to send the image to the printer.

You can print a single image or multiple images. If you work with multiple images, you can print them individually or you can select a layout that prints two or more images per sheet.

① In the Pictures library, select the image or images you want to print.

② Click **Print**.

The Print Pictures dialog box appears.

 If you use more than one printer with your computer, click ⊡ and click the printer you want to use.

 Click ⊡ and click the size of paper you are using.

 Click ⊡ and click the printout quality you prefer.

**Note:** *Print quality is measured in dots per inch (dpi). The higher the dpi value, the better the print quality.*

6 Click the layout you want to use for the printed image.

The Wizard displays a preview of the printout.

7 Click the **Next** button (▶) to see previews of other pages.

8 Click ⬍ to select the number of copies you want.

9 Click **Print**.

The Wizard sends your image or images to the printer.

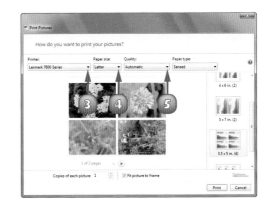

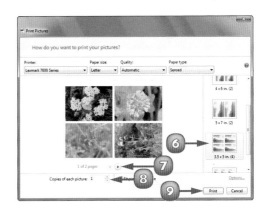

*Photo-quality paper is designed to create a more permanent image and improve the resolution and colour of printed photographs. It comes in a variety of glossy and matte finishes. Be sure to select a paper that your printer manufacturer recommends.*

# CONTENTS

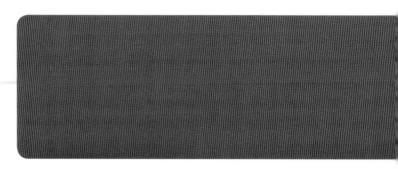

# 5

# PLAYING MUSIC AND OTHER MEDIA

In Windows 7, you play music and other media using the Windows Media Player program. Windows Media Player stores your music files and other media in a special library, and you can use that library to browse your music and display the files by album, artist, genre, and more.

You can also use Windows Media Player to listen to audio files stored on your computer and to play CDs that you insert into your computer CD or DVD drive. Windows Media Player also enables you to watch video files, play DVD discs, and even create your own music CDs.

# OPEN AND CLOSE WINDOWS MEDIA PLAYER

Windows 7 includes Windows Media Player, which is the program you will use throughout this chapter. As you learn in the next few sections, you can use Windows Media Player to navigate your media library, play back and record audio files and music CDs, adjust the volume, as well as view video. To begin using the program, you must first learn how to open the Windows Media Player window.

When you finish using the program, you can close the Windows Media Player window to free up computer processing power.

① Click **Windows Media Player** () in the taskbar.

**Note:** *If you do not see the Media Player icon, you can also click **Start**, click **All Programs**, and then click **Windows Media Player**.*

The first time you start the program, the Welcome to Windows Media Player dialog box appears.

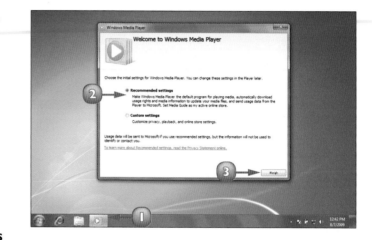

② Click **Recommended settings** (◎ changes to ◉).

③ Click **Finish**.

The Windows Media Player window appears.

④ When you have finished with Media Player, click the **Close** button () to close the window.

The Windows Media Player window closes.

# NAVIGATE THE MEDIA PLAYER WINDOW

The Windows Media Player interface is not complicated, but it does pay to familiarise yourself with the various elements of the Windows Media Player window. This is useful because it helps you get more out of Windows Media Player and it ensures that you can easily navigate and activate elements when you are ready to play audio files or view videos and DVDs.

**A Address Bar**

This area shows your current location in the Media Player library.

**B Tabs**

The tabs are links to the key features of Windows Media Player.

**C Toolbar**

You can use the Media Player toolbar to access commands, change the view, and search for media.

**D Details Pane**

This pane displays information about the contents of the current library location, such as the album art and title, and the title and length of the song or video.

**E Playback Controls**

These buttons control how a video or music file plays and enable you to make adjustments to the sound.

**F Navigation Pane**

You use this pane to navigate the Media Player library's categories.

# USE THE LIBRARY

You can use the library feature in Windows Media Player to manage all of the media files on your computer, including audio files and videos. The library also enables you to organise other digital content, such as music CDs.

When you first start using Windows Media Player, the program automatically updates the library with the files already in your computer's media folders, such as Music and Videos.

## Navigate the Library

**1** In the Navigation pane, click the category you want to use.

**2** If the category includes subcategories, click a subcategory to see its contents.

**3** Double-click the item you want to use.

Media Player displays the contents of the item in the details pane.

**4** You can also click the items in the Address bar to return to a category or subcategory.

**5** Click an arrow to see the contents of any Address bar item.

## Change the Library View

 Click the **View options** ⊡.

 Click the view you want to use.

Media Player changes the view.

---

 *To search the entire library for a specific file, click Library in the Address bar. Otherwise, click the category you want to search. In the search box on the right of the toolbar, type a word or phrase. The matching media appear in the library.*

 *The library automatically groups music into categories based on their media content information, also called metadata or tags. This includes information such as the file type, artist name, song title, rating, play count, and composer.*

# PLAY AN AUDIO OR VIDEO FILE

Windows Media Player uses the library to play audio or video files that you store on your computer. When you select an audio file from a library folder and play it in Windows Media Player, you can switch to the Now Playing window to see a visualisation along with the song. You can also use the Now Playing window to control the playback of the audio or video.

When you want to choose a different song or video, you can switch back to the Windows Media Player library.

① Use the library to navigate to the folder that contains the audio or video file that you want to play.

**Note:** See "Use the Library" to learn more about working with the library's folder.

② Click the audio or video file.

③ Click the **Play** button (▶).

④ Click **Switch to Now Playing** (▦) to view the album art while an audio file plays.

Windows Media Player begins playing the audio or video file.

⑤ Move the mouse ⬏ into the Now Playing window.

The playback buttons appear, which enable you to control how the song or video plays.

**Note:** See "Play a Music CD" to learn more about the playback buttons.

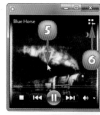

⑥ Click **Switch to Library** (▦) to return to the Media Player library.

# ADJUST THE VOLUME

While an audio or video file is playing, you can adjust the playback volume up or down to get the audio just right. You can adjust the playback volume whether you are playing the audio or video using the Windows Media Player library or the Now Playing window.

If you need to silence the audio or video temporarily, you can mute the playback.

## Adjust the Volume Using the Library

1 Click and drag the **Volume** slider left (to reduce the volume) or right (to increase the volume).

2 If you want to silence the playback, click the **Mute** button (🔊).

**Note:** To restore the volume, click the **Sound** button (🔊).

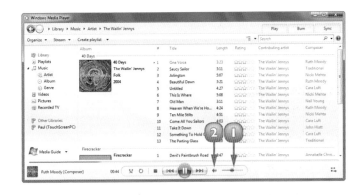

## Adjust the Volume in the Now Playing Window

1 Move the mouse  within the Now Playing window.

The playback controls appear.

2 Click the ⊡ and then drag the **Volume** slider left (to reduce the volume) or right (to increase the volume).

3 To silence the playback, click the **Mute** button (🔊).

**Note:** To restore the volume, click the **Sound** button (🔊).

# PLAY A MUSIC CD

You can play your favourite music CDs in Windows Media Player. You can control some playback options, including skipping a track and pausing and resuming the playback, from the Now Playing window but you can also switch to the Media Player library for more options.

To play a music CD with Windows Media Player, your computer must have a CD or DVD drive.

**1** Insert a music CD into your computer's CD or DVD drive.

**2** Move the mouse ⬚ within the Now Playing window.

The playback controls appear.

## Skip a Track

**3** Click the **Next** button (⏮) to skip to the next track.

**4** Click the **Previous** button (⏭) to skip to the previous track.

## Pause, Resume and Stop Play

**5** Click the **Pause** button (⏸) to pause playback.

**6** Click the **Play** button (▶) to resume playback.

**7** Click the **Stop** button (⏹) to stop playback.

Click the **Play** button (▶) to start the current song again.

**8** Click **Switch to Library** (⊞) to open the Media Player library window.

## Play Another Song

 In the Details pane, double-click the song you want to play.

Windows Media Player begins playing the song.

**A** *This area displays the current song title, the album title, and the song composer.*

## Repeat the CD

**10** Click the **Turn Repeat On** button (⟳).

Windows Media Player restarts the CD after the last track finishes playing.

**Note:** *To turn on repeat from the Now Playing window, press* **Ctrl** + **T**.

## Play Songs Randomly

**11** Click the **Turn Shuffle On** button (⤨).

Windows Media Player shuffles the order of play.

**Note:** *To turn on shuffle from the Now Playing window, press* **Ctrl** + **H**.

> ✓ *You can configure the Now Playing window so that you can control the playback no matter what other programs are running on your PC. Right-click the Now Playing window and then click* **Always show Now Playing on top**.

# COPY TRACKS FROM A MUSIC CD

You can add tracks from a music CD to the library in Windows Media Player. This enables you to listen to an album without having to put the CD into your CD or DVD drive each time. The process of adding tracks from a CD is called **copying,** or **ripping,** in Windows 7.

You can rip an entire CD directly from the Now Playing window or you can rip selected tracks using the library.

## Rip an Entire CD Using the Now Playing Window

 Insert a CD into your computer's CD or DVD drive.

The Now Playing window appears.

 Click **Rip CD** (⚫).

Media Player begins ripping the entire CD.

## Rip Selected Tracks Using the Library

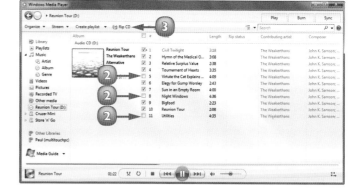

(1) Insert a CD into your computer's CD or DVD drive.

When the Now Playing window appears, click **Switch to Library**.

Media Player displays a list of the CD's tracks.

(2) Click the CD tracks that you do not want to copy (☑ changes to ☐).

(3) Click **Rip CD**.

Windows Media Player begins
copying the track or tracks.

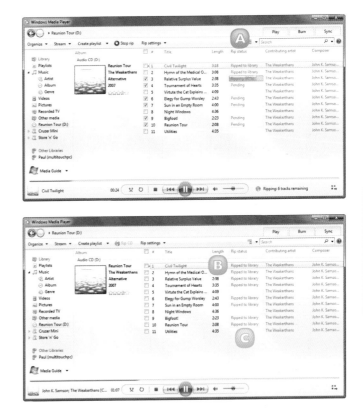

 The Rip Status column displays
the copy progress.

 After each file is copied, the
Rip Status column displays a
Ripped to Library message.

 The copy is complete when
all the tracks you selected
display the Ripped to Library
status.

 **To remove a track from the
library, click Music, click Album,
and then double-click the album
that you ripped to display a list
of the tracks. Right-click the
track that you want to remove
and click Delete.**

 **You can adjust the quality of
the copies by changing the bit
rate, which is a measure of
how much of the CD's original
data gets copied to your
computer. Click Rip Settings,
Audio Quality and then click
the value you want.**

# CREATE A PLAYLIST

You can create a custom music experience by creating your own playlist. Normally, the Windows Media Player library takes the music tracks you copy from a music CD, or the songs you store on your computer hard drive, or download from the Internet, and organises them in preset categories, such as album, artist, and genre. For something different, you can take tracks from multiple categories and add them to a separate playlist, which enables you to play only the songs that you want to hear.

**1** Click **Create playlist**.

Windows Media Player creates a new playlist folder.

**2** Type a name for the new playlist.

**3** Press Esc.

**4** Click and drag items from the library and drop them on the playlist.

**5** Click the playlist.

The Details pane shows the songs you added.

**6** Click and drag the songs to change the playlist order.

**7** Click **Play** (▶) to listen to the playlist.

☑ *By default, Media Player's Navigation pane is configured to show only the five most recent playlists. If you prefer to see all your playlists, right-click any item in the Navigation pane and then click Customize navigation pane. Click the All check box under the Playlists branch (☐ changes to ☑).*

☑ *To add items to an existing playlist, repeat Step 4 for other items. You can also locate the song you want to add, right-click, click Add to, and then click the name of the playlist.*

# BURN MUSIC FILES TO A CD

You can copy, or **burn**, music files from your computer onto a CD. Burning CDs is a great way to create customised CDs that you can listen to on the computer, in your car, through a stereo system, or in a portable device.

With Windows Media Player, you create a list of the songs that you want to add to the CD. You then burn the music files to the CD from within the Windows Media Player window.

To burn music files to a CD with Windows Media Player, your computer must have a recordable CD or DVD drive, and you must have a blank recordable CD disc.

① Insert a blank CD into your computer's recordable CD drive.

② Click the **Burn** tab.

Ⓐ *The Burn list appears.*

③ Click and drag items from the library and drop them inside the Burn list.

Repeat Step **3** to add more files to the Burn list.

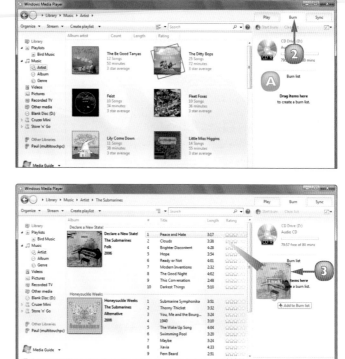

**B** *Windows Media Player adds the files to the Burn list.*

**C** *Windows Media Player updates the approximate time remaining on the disc.*

**4** Click **Start burn**.

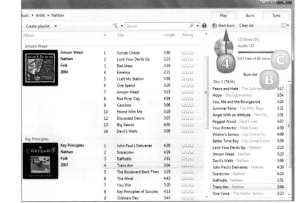

Windows Media Player converts the files to CD tracks and copies them to the CD.

**D** *The Burn tab shows the progress of the burn.*

**Note:** *When the recording is complete, Windows Media Player automatically ejects the disc. Do not attempt to eject the disc yourself before the burn is finished.*

**You can rearrange the tracks before burning. Perhaps the easiest method is to click and drag a track and then drop it in the list location you prefer. You can also click Burn options (⊡▾) and then Shuffle list or Sort list by and then click a sort order.**

**If you have more music than can fit on a single disc, you can still add all the music you want to burn to the Burn list. Windows Media Player fills the first disc and then prompts you to insert a second disc.**

# PLAY A DVD

You can use Windows Media Player to play DVDs. Windows Media Player enables you to watch any multimedia items stored on a DVD, such as movies and video footage.

You can control how a DVD plays by using the controls in the Windows Media Player window, including volume and playback controls. You can also navigate to different scenes using the list of tracks in the Playlist pane. All scenes, or tracks, stem from a root menu that directs you to the DVD's contents.

① Insert a DVD into your computer's DVD drive.

If your DVD begins playing as soon as you insert it, you can skip Steps **2** and **3**.

② In Windows Media Player, click the DVD in the Navigation pane.

③ Click **Play** (▶).

Windows Media Player plays the DVD and displays the DVD's menu.

Ⓐ *DVD menu items can vary in appearance and use different layouts.*

④ Click the menu item or feature you want to access.

Windows Media Player begins playback.

To control playback, position the mouse ▷ within the DVD window.

Windows Media Player displays the playback controls.

## Stop and Start a DVD

**6** Click the **Stop** button (■) to stop the DVD playback.

**7** Click the **Play** button (▶) to restart the playback from the beginning.

**8** You can click the **Pause** button (⏸) to pause the playback if you want to resume playing (▶) in the same scene.

## Navigate Scenes

**9** Click the **Previous** button (⏮) to jump to the previous scene.

**10** Click the **Next** button (⏭) to jump to the next scene.

**11** You can also rewind or fast-forward the DVD by clicking and dragging the **Seek** slider.

## Use the DVD Options

**12** Click the **DVD** ▾.

Windows Media Player displays a list of DVD options.

You can use the DVD options to return to the main menu, select special features, and display the DVD full-screen.

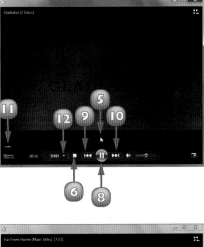

**13** Click **Root menu**.

The DVD's opening menu appears in the Windows Media Player window.

 *The root menu typically displays links to the various segments, features, or clips on the DVD. In full-screen view, right-click on the DVD screen, click DVD features, and then click Root menu.*

# CONTENTS

# 6

## WORKING WITH FILES

This chapter shows you how to work with the files on your computer. These easy and efficient methods show you how to perform the most common file tasks, including viewing files, selecting files, copying and moving files, and renaming files. In this chapter you also learn how to burn files to a recordable CD or DVD disc and how to create new folders to hold your files. You also learn how to delete a file that you no longer need, as well as how to restore a file that you deleted accidentally. Finally, you also learn how to use Windows 7's powerful search feature to help you locate the file you need.

# VIEW YOUR FILES

You can view the files you create, as well as those stored on your hard drive that you download and copy to your computer. All your files are stored in folders on your computer's hard drive. Some of your files will be in the main libraries that are part of your user profile – including Documents, Music, and Pictures – but you may have other files within subfolders of those libraries.

If you want to open or work with those files, you first need to open the appropriate library or subfolder to view them.

① Click **Start**.

② Click your user name.

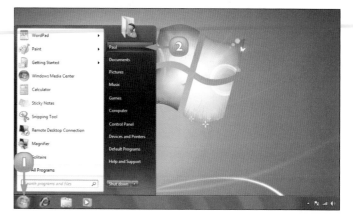

Windows 7 displays your user folder.

③ Double-click the folder you want to view.

Windows 7 displays the contents of the folder including subfolders.

4 If the files you want to view are stored in a subfolder, double-click the subfolder.

Windows 7 displays the contents of the subfolder.

**To view files on removable media, insert the media into the appropriate drive or slot on your computer. If you see the AutoPlay window, click Open folder to view files. Otherwise, click Start, Computer and then double-click the device that contains the files you want to view.**

**In Windows 7, the four main document storage areas — Documents, Music, Pictures, and Videos — are set up as libraries, consisting of two or more folders. For example, the Documents library contains My Documents and Public Documents. To add a folder to a library, click the locations link and then click Add.**

# SELECT A FILE

Whether you want to rename a file, make a copy of a file, move several files to a new location, or delete some files, you first have to select the file or files so that Windows 7 knows exactly the ones you want to work with.

Although you learn specifically about selecting files in this section, the technique for selecting folders is exactly the same.

## Select a Single File

1. Open the folder containing the file.

2. Click the file.

## Select Multiple Files

1. Open the folder containing the files.

2. Click the first file you want to select.

3. Press and hold **Ctrl** and click each of the other files you want to select.

## Select a Group of Files

1. Open the folder containing the files.

2. Position the mouse ⬚ slightly above and slightly to the left of the first file in the group.

3. Click and drag the mouse ⬚ down and to the right until all the files in the group are selected.

## Select All Files

1. Open the folder containing the files.

2. Click **Organize**.

3. Click **Select all**.

   Windows Explorer selects all the files in the folder.

**Note:** *A quick way to select all the files in a folder is to press* Ctrl + A.

> ☑ *To deselect a single file from a multiple-file selection, press and hold* Ctrl *and click the file you want to deselect. To deselect all files, click an empty area within the folder. To reverse a selection – swap the selected and deselected files – click* **Edit, Invert Selection.**

# CHANGE THE FILE VIEW

You can configure how Windows 7 displays the files in a folder by changing the file view. This enables you to see larger or smaller icons or the details of each file.

Choose a view such as Small Icons to see more files in the folder window. For files that show preview thumbnails instead of icons – such as pictures and videos – choose a view such as Large Icons or Extra Large Icons to get a better look at the thumbnails.

If you want to see more information about the files, choose either Tiles view or Details view.

① Open the folder containing the files you want to view.

② Click the **Views** ⊡ to open the Views list.

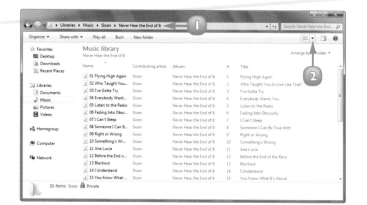

③ Click the view you want.

Ⓐ *The slider points to the current view. You can also click and drag the slider to select a view.*

Windows Explorer changes the file view (to Tiles, in this example).

# PREVIEW A FILE

Windows 7 enables you to view the contents of some files without opening them. This makes it easier to select the file you want to work with.

One way to preview a file is to switch to a view that shows preview thumbnails, such as Large Icons or Extra Large Icons. However, to get a larger preview and to preview a wider variety of file types, you need to open Windows Explorer's Preview pane.

Windows 7 previews only certain types of files, such as text documents, rich text documents, Web pages, images, and videos.

① Open the folder containing the file you want to preview.

② Click the **Preview pane** icon (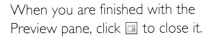).

The Preview pane appears.

Ⓐ *The file's contents appear in the Preview pane.*

③ You can click and drag the left border of the Preview pane to change its size.

④ When you are finished with the Preview pane, click 🔲 to close it.

# COPY A FILE

You can make an exact copy of a file, which is useful if you want to make a backup of an important file on a flash drive, memory card, or other removable disk, or if you want to send the copy on a disk to another person.

This section shows you how to copy a single file, but the steps also work if you select multiple files, as described earlier in this chapter in the "Select a File" section. You can also use these steps to copy a folder.

**①** Open the folder containing the file you want to copy.

**②** Select the file.

**③** Click **Organize**.

**④** Click **Copy**.

Windows 7 places a copy of the file in a special memory location called the *clipboard*.

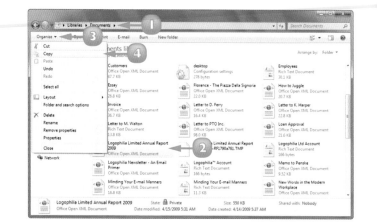

**⑤** Open the location you want to use to store the copy.

**⑥** Click **Organize**.

**⑦** Click **Paste**.

**Ⓐ** *Windows 7 inserts a copy of the file in the location.*

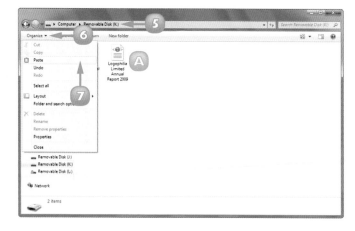

# MOVE A FILE

When you need to store a file in a new location, the easiest way is to move the file from its current folder to another folder on your computer.

This section shows you how to move a single file, but the steps also work if you select multiple files, as described earlier in this chapter in the "Select a File" section. You can also use these steps to move a folder.

1. Open the folder containing the file you want to move.

2. Select the file.

3. Click **Organize**.

4. Click **Cut**.

   Windows 7 removes the file from the folder and places it in a special memory location called the *clipboard*.

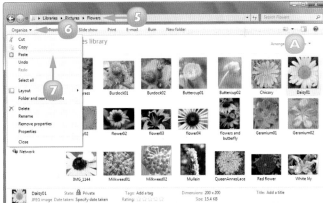

5. Click the new location you want to use for the file.

6. Click **Organize**.

7. Click **Paste**.

   Ⓐ *Windows 7 inserts the file in the new location.*

# BURN FILES TO A CD OR DVD

If your computer has a recordable CD or DVD drive, you can copy – or **burn** – files and folders to a recordable disc. This enables you to store a large amount of data in a single place for convenient transport, storage or backup.

To burn files, your computer must have a recordable CD or DVD drive and you must have a blank recordable CD or DVD disc.

If you want to copy music files to a CD, see the "Burn Music Files to a CD" section in Chapter 5.

① Insert a recordable disc into your recordable CD or DVD drive.

The AutoPlay dialog box appears.

② Click **Burn files to disc**.

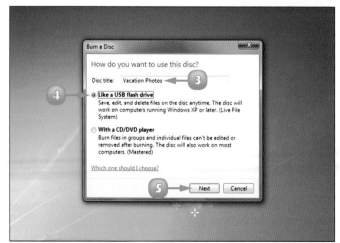

If you have never used the disc for burning files, the Burn a Disc dialog box appears.

③ Type a title for the disc.

④ Click **Like a USB flash drive** (◎ changes to ◉).

⑤ Click **Next**.

Windows 7 formats the disc and displays a dialog box to show you the progress.

⑥ Click **Close** (⊠) when the format is complete and the AutoPlay dialog box appears.

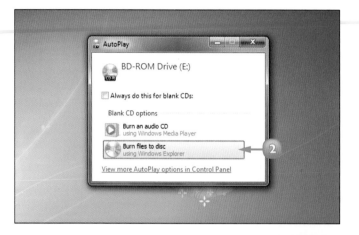

**7** Open the folder containing the files you want to copy to the disc.

**8** Select the files.

**A** If you selected more than 15 files and you want to see the total size of the selection, click **Show more details**. The Size in the Details pane shows the total size of the selected files.

**9** Click **Burn**.

**Note:** If you want to copy everything in the folder to the disc, do not select any file or folder and click **Burn**.

Windows 7 burns the files to the disc.

Windows 7 opens the disc and displays the copied files.

**10** Repeat Steps **7** to **9** to burn more files to the disc.

**11** Open the disc folder.

**12** Click **Close session**.

Windows 7 closes the disc session to allow the disc to be used on other computers.

**B** This message appears while the disc is being closed.

**13** When the Closing Session message disappears, click **Eject**.

Windows 7 ejects the disc.

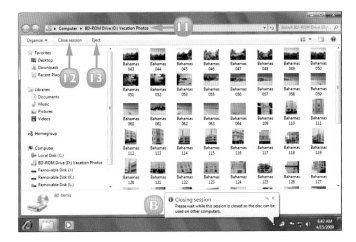

 **To erase and reuse a disc, click Start, Computer. Right-click the disc icon and click Format. Type a new name for the disc, if desired, in the Format dialog box and click Start.**

# RENAME A FILE

You can change the names of your files, which is useful if the current name of a file does not accurately describe its contents. By giving your documents descriptive names, you make it easier to find the file you want.

Make sure that you rename only those documents that you have created yourself or that someone else has given to you. Do not rename any of the Windows 7 system files or any files associated with your programs, or your computer may behave erratically or crash.

**1** Open the folder that contains the file you want to rename.

**2** Click the file.

**3** Click **Organize**.

**Note:** *In addition to renaming files, you can also rename any folders that you create yourself.*

**4** Click **Rename**.

A text box appears around the file name.

**Note:** *You can also select the Rename command by clicking the file and then pressing* F2.

**5** Type the new name you want to use for the file.

**Note:** *The name you type can be up to 255 characters long, but it cannot include the following characters:* < > , ? : " \ *.

**Note:** *To abort renaming the file, press* Esc *to cancel the operation.*

**6** Press Enter or click an empty section of the folder.

The new name appears under the file's icon.

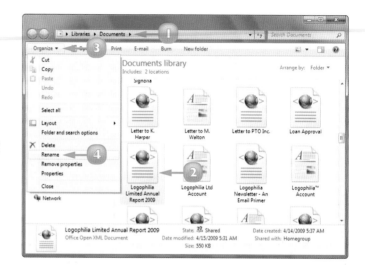

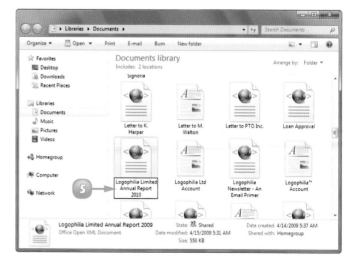

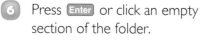

# CREATE A NEW FILE

You can quickly create a new file directly within a file folder. You normally create a new file by opening the appropriate programs, pulling down the File menu, and then choosing the New command, as explained in the "Create a Document" section in Chapter 3. However, creating a new file directly within a folder is faster, and often more convenient, than running a program's New command because you do not need to open a program to create the file.

 Open the folder in which you want to create the file.

② Right-click an empty section of the folder.

③ Click **New**.

④ Click the type of file you want to create.

**Note:** *If you click* **Folder**, *Windows 7 creates a new subfolder.*

**Note:** *The New menu on your system may contain more items than you see here because some programs install their own file types.*

Ⓐ *An icon for the new file appears in the folder.*

⑤ Type the name you want to use for the new file.

⑥ Press Enter.

# DELETE A FILE

When you have a file that you no longer need, instead of leaving the file to clutter your hard drive, you can delete it.

Make sure that you delete only those documents that you have created yourself or that someone else has given to you. Do not delete any of the Windows 7 system files or any files associated with your programs, or your computer may behave erratically or crash.

If you happen to delete a file accidentally, you can usually recover it.

① Open the folder that contains the file you want to delete.

② Click the file you want to delete.

**Note:** *If you need to remove more than one file, select all the files you want to delete.*

③ Click **Organize**.

④ Click **Delete**.

**Note:** *Another way to select the Delete command is to press* Del.

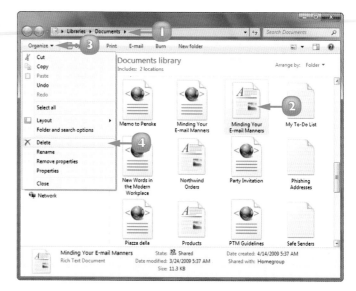

The Delete File dialog box appears.

⑤ Click **Yes**.

The file disappears from the folder.

**Note:** *Another way to delete a file is to click and drag it to the desktop's Recycle Bin icon.*

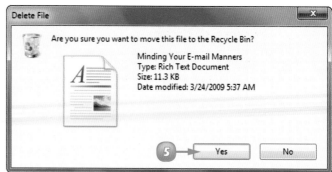

# RESTORE A DELETED FILE

If you delete a file in error, Windows 7 enables you to restore the file by placing it back in the folder from which you deleted it.

You can restore a deleted file because Windows 7 moves each deleted file from its original folder to a special folder called the Recycle Bin, where the file stays for a few days or a few weeks, depending on how often you empty the Recycle Bin or how full the folder becomes.

① Double-click the desktop **Recycle Bin** icon.

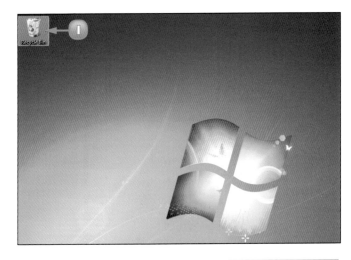

The Recycle Bin folder appears.

② Click the file you want to restore.

③ Click **Restore this item**.

The file disappears from the Recycle Bin and reappears in its original folder.

# SEARCH FOR A FILE

After you have used your computer for a while and have created many documents, you might have trouble locating a specific file. This is particularly true if you use your computer frequently, because you might have thousands of your own files stored in various folders throughout the hard drive. You can save a great deal of time by having Windows 7 search for your document.

Windows 7 searches not only for documents, but also for e-mail messages, contacts, Internet Explorer favorites, applications, and more.

## Search from the Start Menu

① Click **Start**.

② Click the Search box and type your search text.

    Ⓐ *As you type, Windows 7 displays the programs, documents, and other data on your system with a name that matches your search text.*

③ If you see the program or document you want, click it to open it.

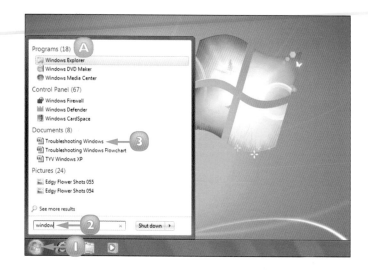

## Search from a Folder Window

① Open the folder in which you want to search.

② Click the Search box.

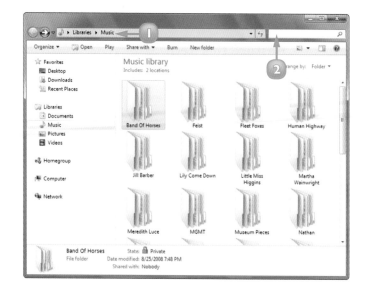

3 Type your search text.

A As you type, Windows 7 displays the folders and documents in the current folder with names, contents, or keywords that match your search text.

4 If you see the folder or document you want, double-click it to open it.

## Save a Search

1 Run the search you want to save.

2 Click **Save Search**.

The Save As dialog box appears.

3 Type a file name for the search.

4 Click **Save**.

Windows 7 saves the search file in the Favorites area. Click the file to rerun your search.

# CONTENTS

# SHARING YOUR COMPUTER WITH OTHERS

If you share your computer with other people, you can create separate user accounts so that each person works only with his own documents, programs, and Windows 7 settings. This chapter shows you how to view and create user accounts, log on and off different accounts, change a user's name and picture, and delete accounts you no longer need.

In this chapter you also learn about Windows 7's homegroup feature, which makes it easy to share documents, music, photos and other files with people on your network.

# DISPLAY USER ACCOUNTS

To create, change, or delete user accounts, you need to display Windows 7's Manage Accounts window.

If you share your computer with other people, you can run into problems because each person wants his own programs, documents, and settings. To solve these problems, you can create a separate user account for each person. A *user account* is a kind of profile that Windows 7 maintains for a single person. That profile gives each user his own collection of folders and settings, and allows each user to install his own programs. When a person logs into his account, he does not see the profile of any other user.

**①** Click **Start**.

**②** Click **Control Panel**.

The Control Panel window appears.

**③** Click **Add or remove user accounts**.

**Note:** *If the User Account Control dialog box appears, click **Continue** or type an administrator password and click **Submit**.*

The Manage Accounts window appears.

**Ⓐ** *An administrator account is created when you install Windows 7. When you start Windows 7, you log on with this account.*

**Ⓑ** *The Guest account is a limited permission account. To turn on the Guest account, click **Guest** and then click **Turn On**.*

**④** Click the **Close** button (☒) to close the Manage Accounts window.

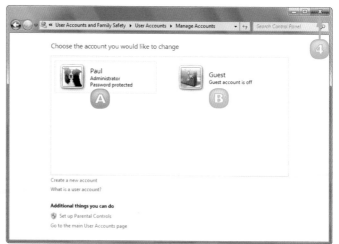

# CREATE A USER ACCOUNT

If you want to share your computer with another person, you need to create a user account for that individual. If you supply a password with an account, then only people who know that password can access the account's files, programs, and settings. This is an excellent security precaution, so you should safeguard each account with a password.

Note that you must be logged on to Windows 7 with an administrator account or know an administrator's password to create a user account.

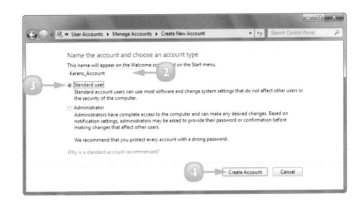

① In the Manage Accounts window, click Create a new account.

② Type the name you want to use for the new account.

③ Click the account type you want (◯ changes to ◉).

④ Click **Create Account**.

Windows 7 creates the user account.

## Create a Password

① Click the user account.

② Click **Create a password**.

③ Type the password.

The password characters appear as dots for security reasons.

④ Type the password again.

⑤ Type a hint that will help you or the user remember the password.

⑥ Click **Create password**.

Windows 7 adds the password to the account.

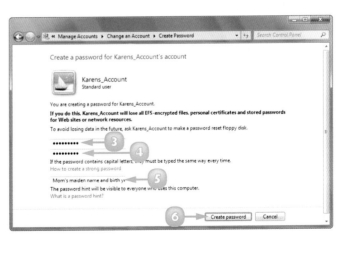

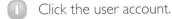

# SWITCH BETWEEN ACCOUNTS

After you have created more than one account on your computer, you can switch between accounts. This is useful when one person is already working in Windows 7 and another person needs to use the computer.

One way to do this would be to have the current user log off and then have the other user log on. This works, but it is often inconvenient, particularly if the original user wants to resume working when the other user is finished with the computer.

To avoid this problem, you can switch from one account to another. In this case, Windows 7 leaves the original user's programs and windows running so that after the second person is finished, the original user can log on again and continue working as before.

1 Click **Start**.

A The current user's name and picture appear on the Start menu.

2 Click the power button arrow (▶) to display the menu.

3 Click **Switch user**.

The Welcome screen appears.

4 Click the user account you want to switch to.

If the account is protected by a password, the password box appears.

**Note:** See "Protect an Account with a Password" in Chapter 10 for more details.

 Type the password.

6 Click the **Go** button ().

7 Click **Start**.

The Start menu now shows:

(A) the user's name

(B) the user's picture

When you set up your password, Windows 7 asks you to supply a hint to help you remember the password. If you cannot remember your password, click the **Go button** (). Click **OK** to return to the Welcome screen and Windows 7 displays the password hint.

# CHANGE A USER'S NAME

If the user name you are using now is not suitable for some reason, you can change to a different name. If you are running Windows 7 under an administrator account, then you can also change the name of any other user on the system.

When you change the user's name, you are changing the name that appears on the Start menu, in the Manage Accounts window, and on the Windows 7 Welcome screen.

① Display the Manage Accounts window.

**Note:** See "Display User Accounts," earlier in this chapter, to learn how to display the Manage Accounts window.

② Click the user account you want to work with.

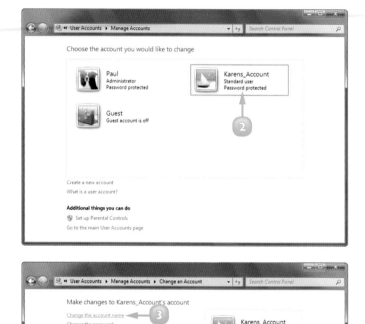

The Change an Account window appears.

③ Click **Change the account name**.

The Rename Account window appears.

④ Type the new name.

**Note:** *The name cannot be any longer than 20 characters and cannot include any of the following characters:* , < > / ? ; : " [ ] \ | = + *

**Note:** *The name cannot be the same as the computer's name.*

⑤ Click **Change Name**.

Ⓐ *The new name appears in the user's window.*

⑥ Click **Manage another account** to return to the Manage Accounts window.

☑ **To check the computer name, click Start, Control Panel, System and Security, and See the name of this computer. In the System window, look for the Computer Name setting.**

# CHANGE A USER'S PICTURE

Windows 7 assigns a random picture to each new user account. This picture appears in the Manage Accounts window, the Welcome screen, and on the Start menu. If you do not like your picture or if you have a more suitable picture that you would prefer to use, you can change your picture. You can either use one of the three dozen pictures that Windows 7 provides or you can use one of your own pictures, such as a photo or drawing.

① Display the Manage Accounts window.

**Note:** See "Display User Accounts", earlier in this chapter, to learn how to display the Manage Accounts window.

② Click the user account you want to work with.

The Change an Account window appears.

③ Click **Change the picture**.

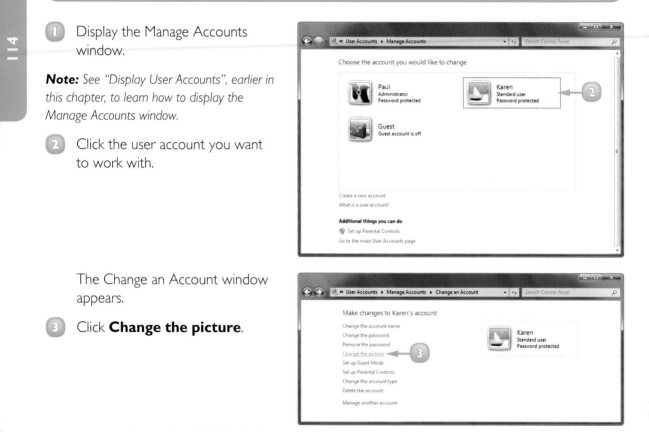

The Choose Picture window appears.

④ To use one of your own pictures, click **Browse for more pictures**.

The Open dialog box appears.

⑤ Open the folder containing the picture you want to use.

⑥ Click the picture.

⑦ Click **Open** to use that picture or **Cancel** to return to the standard pictures.

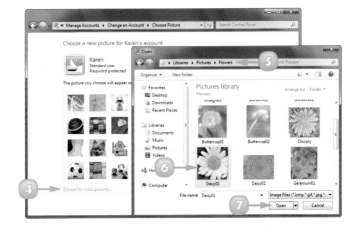

The Choose Picture window appears.

⑧ Click the picture you want to use.

⑨ Click **Change Picture**.

Choose a new picture for Karen's account

Karen
Standard user
Password protected

The picture you choose will appear on the Welcome screen and on the Start menu.

Browse for more pictures...

Change Picture    Cancel

The user's window appears and displays the new picture.

# DELETE AN ACCOUNT

You can delete a user's account when it is no longer needed. This reduces the number of users in the Manage Accounts window and on the Welcome screen, which makes those screens easier to navigate.

Deleting an account can also free up some disk space. When you delete an account, Windows 7 asks if you want to keep the user's files on the computer, including the user's documents, music, pictures, and video. If you choose not to keep those files, Windows 7 deletes them from the hard drive, thus freeing up the disk space they used.

① Display the Manage Accounts window.

**Note:** See "Display User Accounts", earlier in this chapter, to learn how to display the Manage Accounts window.

② Click the user account you want to delete.

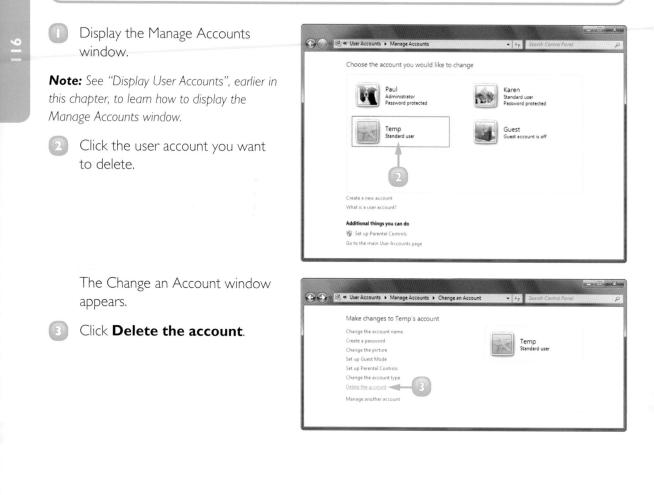

The Change an Account window appears.

③ Click **Delete the account**.

The Delete Account window appears.

④ Click to specify whether you want to keep or delete the user's personal files.

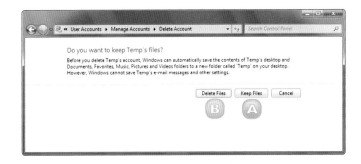

Ⓐ *Click Keep Files to retain the user's personal files. The contents of the Documents folder and desktop are saved on your desktop in a folder named after the user. All other personal items – settings, e-mail accounts and messages, and Internet Explorer favorites – are deleted.*

Ⓑ *Click Delete Files to delete all of the user's personal files, settings, messages, and favorites.*

The Confirm Deletion window appears.

⑤ Click **Delete Account**.

Windows 7 deletes the account.

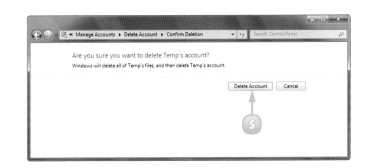

🛑 *If yours is the only administrator account left on the computer, Windows 7 does not allow you to delete it. Windows 7 requires that there is always at least one administrator account on the computer.*

# CREATE A HOMEGROUP

You can share documents and media easily with other Windows 7 computers by creating a homegroup on your network. A homegroup simplifies network sharing by making it easy to share documents, pictures, music, videos, and even printers.

You use one Windows 7 computer to create the homegroup and assign it a password. You then use the password to join your other Windows 7 computers to the homegroup.

① Click **Start**.

② Click **Documents**.

The Documents library appears.

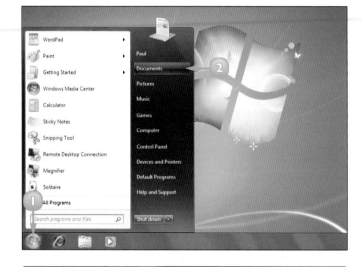

③ Click **Homegroup**.

④ Click **Create a homegroup**.

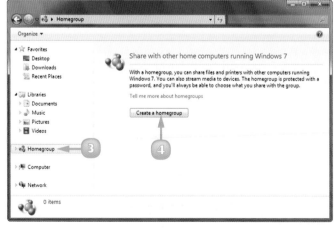

The Create a Homegroup Wizard appears.

⑤ Click the check box for each type of file you want to share with the homegroup (☐ changes to ☑).

⑥ Click **Next**.

Windows 7 creates the homegroup.

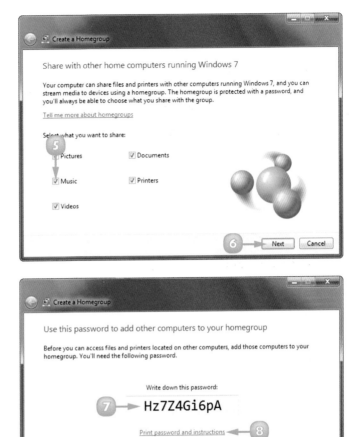

The Create a Homegroup Wizard displays the homegroup password.

⑦ Write down the homegroup password.

⑧ Alternatively, you can click to print the password.

⑨ Click **Finish**.

You can now join your other Windows 7 computers to the homegroup.

☑ *If you lose the homegroup password, click Start, Control Panel. Under Network and Internet, click Choose homegroup and sharing options. Click the View or print homegroup password link to see your password.*

# CONNECT TO A WIRELESS NETWORK

If you have a wireless access point in your home or office, and you have a wireless network adapter installed on your computer, you can connect to the access point to access your network. If your wireless access point is connected to the Internet, then connecting to the wireless network gives your computer Internet access, as well.

Most wireless networks are protected with a security key, which is a kind of password. If your wireless network requires a security key, be sure you know the key before attempting to connect.

① Click the **Network** icon (◢) in the taskbar's notification area.

Windows 7 displays a list of wireless networks in your area.

Ⓐ *Windows 7 displays the Unsecured icon (▨) for networks not protected by a security key.*

② Click your network.

③ To have Windows 7 connect to your network automatically in the future, click the **Connect automatically** check box (☐ changes to ☑).

④ Click **Connect**.

If the network is protected by a security key, Windows 7 displays the Connect to a Network window.

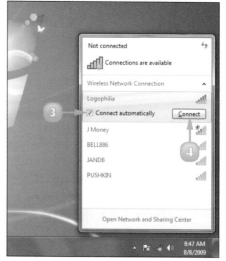

Type the security key.

**Note:** *If you are worried that someone nearby might see the security key, you can click **Hide characters** ( changes to ) to display the characters you type as dots.*

 Click **OK**.

Windows 7 connects to the network.

Ⓐ *The network icon changes from ▨ to ▨ to indicate that you now have a wireless network connection.*

## To Disconnect from a Wireless Network

① Click the **Network** icon (▨).

② Click your network.

③ Click **Disconnect**.

Windows 7 disconnects from the wireless network.

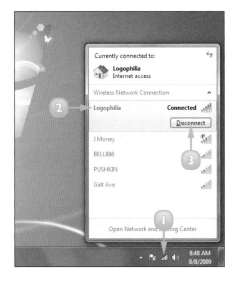

# CONTENTS

# 8

After you have your Internet connection up and running,
you can use Windows 7's Internet Explorer program to
navigate – or *surf* – the sites of the World Wide Web. This
chapter explains the Web and shows you how to navigate
from site to site by selecting links and entering Web page
addresses. You also learn how to open pages in tabs and
return to pages you have visited previously. This chapter also
shows you how to change your home page, save your
favourite pages for easier access later and search for
information on the Web.

# UNDERSTANDING THE WORLD WIDE WEB

The World Wide Web – the Web, for short – is a massive storehouse of information that resides on computers, called *Web servers,* located all over the world. Each Web server hosts one or more Web sites, and each of those sites contains dozens, hundreds, or even thousands of documents called *pages.*

You navigate from site to site and from page to page by clicking special words, phrases, or images called *links,* or by entering the address of the site or page you want to view. You do all of this using a special software program called a *Web browser.*

## Web Page

World Wide Web information is presented on Web pages, which you download to your computer using a Web browser program, such as Windows 7's Internet Explorer. Each Web page can combine text with images, sounds, music, and even video. The Web consists of billions of pages covering almost every imaginable topic.

## Web Site

A Web site is a collection of Web pages associated with a particular person, business, government, school, or organization. Web sites are stored on a Web server, a special computer that makes Web pages available for people to browse.

## Web Address

Every Web page has its own Web address that uniquely identifies the page. This address is sometimes called a *URL* (pronounced *yoo-ar-ell* or *erl*), which is short for Uniform Resource Locator. If you know the address of a page, you can plug that address into your Web browser to view the page.

## Links

A *link* (also called a hyperlink) is a kind of "cross-reference" to another Web page. Each link is a bit of text (usually shown underlined and in a different colour) or an image that, when you click it, loads the other page into your Web browser automatically. The other page is often from the same site, but it is common to come across links that take you to pages anywhere on the Web.

# START INTERNET EXPLORER

You can use Internet Explorer, Windows 7's built-in Web browser program, to surf the Web. To do this, you must first start Internet Explorer. When you have completed your work on the Web, you should shut down Internet Explorer to reduce clutter on your screen and recover some system resources.

Some versions of Windows 7, particularly those sold in the European Union, do not include the Internet Explorer Web browser. To obtain Internet Explorer, contact your computer manufacturer or Microsoft.

**①** Connect to the Internet.

**②** Click **Internet Explorer**.

**Note:** *If you do not see the Internet Explorer icon in the taskbar, click* **Start**, **All Programs**, *and then* **Internet Explorer**.

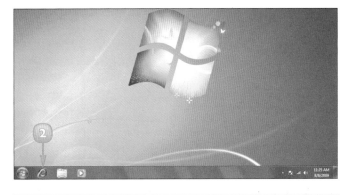

The Internet Explorer window appears.

**Note:** *If you see the Welcome to Internet Explorer 8 dialog box, click* **Next**, **Use express settings** *(◎ changes to ◉), and then* **Finish**.

**③** When you are finished with the Web, click the **Close** button (⊠) to shut down Internet Explorer.

# NAVIGATE INTERNET EXPLORER

If your computer is running Windows, then your default Web browser is most likely Internet Explorer. This is Microsoft's browser and it comes with most versions of Windows, which is part of the reason why it is the most popular browser in use today.

This section introduces you to the main features of the Internet Explorer window. You can more easily surf the Web if you know your way around the Internet Explorer Web browser.

### Ⓐ Web Page Title

This part of the Internet Explorer title bar displays the title of the displayed Web page.

### Ⓑ Address Bar

This text box displays the address of the displayed Web page. You can also use the address bar to type the address of a Web page that you want to visit.

### Ⓒ Links

Links appear either as text or as images. On most pages (although not the page shown here), text links appear underlined and in a different colour (usually blue) from the regular page text.

### Ⓓ Current Link

This is the link that you are currently pointing at with your mouse. The mouse pointer changes from ☖ to ☝. On some pages, the link text also becomes underlined (as shown here) and changes colour.

### Ⓔ Status Bar

This area displays the current status of Internet Explorer. For example, it displays "Opening page" when you are downloading a Web page and "Done" when the page is fully loaded. When you point at a link, the status bar displays the address of the page associated with the link.

# SELECT A LINK

Almost all Web pages include links to other pages that contain information related to something in the current page and you can use these links to navigate to other Web pages. When you select a link, your Web browser loads the other page.

Knowing which words, phrases or images are links is not always obvious. The only way to tell for sure in many cases is to position the ⊳ over the text or image; if the ⊳ changes to a ⊘, you know you are dealing with a link.

① Position the ⊳ over the link (⊳ changes to ⊘).

② Click the text or image.

The status bar shows the current download status.

**Note:** *The address shown in the status bar when you point at a link may be different from the one shown when the page is downloading. This happens when the Web site "redirects" the link, which happens frequently.*

The linked Web page appears.

Ⓐ *The Web page title and address change after the linked page is loaded.*

Ⓑ *The status bar shows Done when the page is completely loaded.*

# ENTER A WEB PAGE ADDRESS

If you know the address of a specific Web page, you can type that address into the Web browser and the program will display the page.

Internet Explorer's Address bar also doubles as a list of the Web page addresses you have entered most recently. By pulling down that list you can see these recent addresses and select one to return to that site.

## Type a Web Page Address

① Click in the address bar.

② Type the address of the Web page.

**Note:** *Most Web addresses begin with http://. You can leave off these characters when you type your address; Internet Explorer adds them automatically.*

**Note:** *If the address uses the form www. something.com, type just the "something" part and press* Ctrl + Enter. *Internet Explorer automatically adds http://www. at the beginning and .com at the end.*

③ Click the **Go** button (⊡) or press Enter.

The Web page appears.

## Redisplay a Web Page

 Click ⊡ in the address bar.

A list of the addresses you have typed appears.

② Click the address you want to display.

The Web page appears.

**Note:** *If you type the first few letters of the address (such as* **goog***), the address bar displays a list of addresses that match what you have typed. If you see the address you want, click it to load the page.*

**STOP** *If Internet Explorer says "The page cannot be displayed", it means that Internet Explorer is unable to contact a Web server at the address you typed. This is often a temporary glitch, so click Refresh (⟳) to try loading the page again. If the trouble persists, double-check the address to ensure that you typed it correctly. If you did, the site may be unavailable for some reason. Try again in a few hours.*

# OPEN A WEB PAGE IN A TAB

You can make it easier to work with multiple Web pages simultaneously by opening each page in its own tab.

When you use a Web browser normally, each page appears in the main part of the browser window, which is usually called the content area. A tab is like a second content area and it appears "behind" the first one, with only a small tab (hence the name) visible. Click the tab and you see the second content area and its loaded Web page. You can open as many pages as you want in their own tabs. This is convenient because all the pages appear within a single Internet Explorer window.

① Right-click the link you want to open.

② Click **Open in New Tab**.

A new tab appears with the page title.

③ Click the tab to display the page.

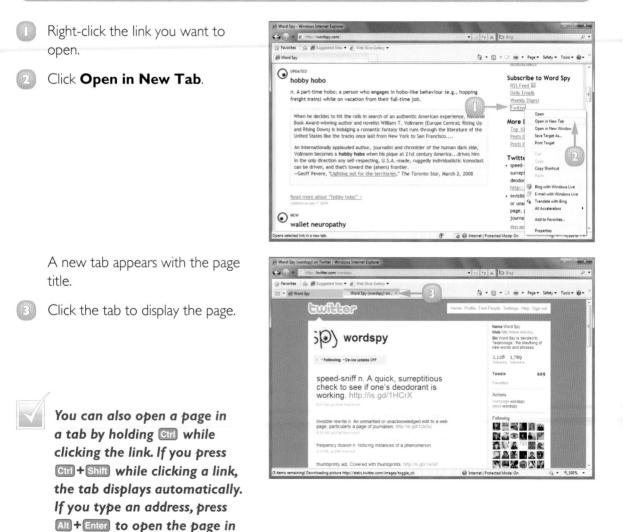

✓ **You can also open a page in a tab by holding Ctrl while clicking the link. If you press Ctrl + Shift while clicking a link, the tab displays automatically. If you type an address, press Alt + Enter to open the page in new tab.**

## Navigate Tabs

 Click the **Tab Left** button (⊞) or the **Tab Right** button (⊞) to display the tab you want.

*Note: You see the Tab Left and Tab Right buttons only if Internet Explorer does not have enough room to display all the tabs.*

 Click the tab.

The Web page loaded in the tab appears.

## Display Quick Tabs

 Click the **Quick Tabs** button (⊞).

Internet Explorer displays thumbnail images of the Web pages open in each tab.

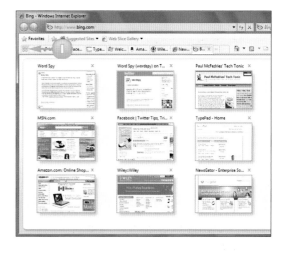

*You can also press Ctrl+Q to display the Quick Tabs. Press Ctrl+Tab or Ctrl+Shift+Tab to cycle through the tabs. Press Ctrl+W to close the current tab and press Ctrl+Alt+F4 to close every tab but the current one.*

# NAVIGATE WEB PAGES

After you have visited several pages, you can return to a page you visited earlier. Instead of making you retype the address or look for the link, Internet Explorer gives you some easier methods.

When you navigate Web pages, you can go back to a page you have visited in the current browser session. After you have done that, you can reverse course and go forward through the pages again.

## Go Back One Page

**1** Click the **Back** button (◀).

The previous page you visited appears.

## Go Back Several Pages

**1** Click the **Recent Pages** ▾.

A list of the sites you have visited appears.

**A** *The current site appears with a check mark (☑) beside it.*

**B** *Items listed below the current site are ones you visited prior to the current site.*

**C** *When you position the mouse ◊ over a previous site, Internet Explorer displays the Go Back arrow (◀).*

**2** Click the page you want to display.

The page appears.

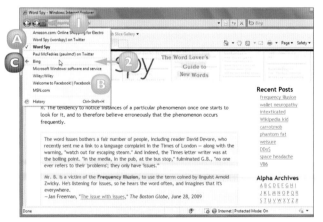

## Go Forward One Page

 Click the **Forward** button ().

The next page you visited appears.

**Note:** *If you are at the last page viewed up to that point, the Forward button (▸) is not active.*

## Go Forward Several Pages

⬤ Click the **Recent Pages** ▾.

A list of the sites you have visited appears.

Ⓐ *Items listed above the current site are ones you visited after the current site.*

Ⓑ *When you position the mouse ⬚ over a previous site, Internet Explorer displays the Go Forward arrow (▸).*

② Click the page you want to display.

The page appears.

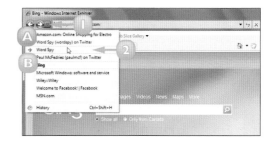

## Keep Several Pages on Screen

⬤ Press Ctrl + N.

A new Internet Explorer window appears.

② Use the techniques described in this section to navigate to the page you want.

# CHANGE YOUR HOME PAGE

Your home page is the Web page that appears when you first start Internet Explorer. The default home page is usually the MSN.com site, but you can change that to any other page you want. For example, many people prefer to open a search engine page at start up.

In the Windows 7 version of Internet Explorer, you can have a single home page or you can have multiple home pages that load in separate tabs each time you start the program.

## Change a Single Home Page

1. Display the Web page that you want to use as your home page.

2. Click the **Home** button (⏷).

3. Click **Add or Change Home Page**.

The Add or Change Home Page dialog box appears.

4. Click **Use this webpage as your only home page** (◎ changes to ◉).

5. Click **Yes**.

Internet Explorer changes your home page.

 You can click the **Home** button (🏠) to display the home page at any time.

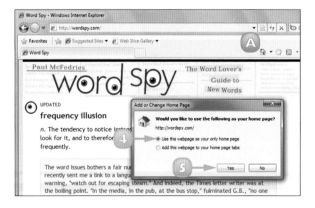

## Add a Page to Your Home Page Tabs

1. Display the Web page that you want to add to your home page tabs.

2. Click the **Home** button ⊡.

3. Click **Add or Change Home Page**.

   The Add or Change Home Page dialog box appears.

4. Click **Add this webpage to your home page tabs** (◎ changes to ◉).

5. Click **Yes**.

   Internet Explorer adds the page to your home page tabs.

   A. You can click the **Home** button (🏠) to display home page tabs at any time.

**Note:** To return to using your original home page, click **Tools**, **Internet Options**. Click the **General** tab, click **Use default**, and then click **OK**.

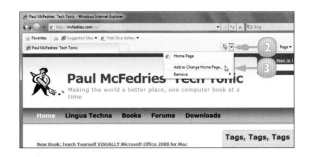

**To get Internet Explorer to load without displaying a home page, click Tools, Internet Options, Use blank, OK.**

# SAVE FAVOURITE WEB PAGES

If you have Web pages that you visit frequently, you can save yourself time by saving those pages as favourites within Internet Explorer. This enables you to display the pages with just a couple of mouse clicks.

The Favorites feature is a list of Web pages that you have saved. Instead of typing an address or searching for one of these pages, you can display the Web page by selecting its address from the Favorites list.

① Display the Web page you want to save as a favourite.

② Click the **Favorites Center** button (⬚).

③ Click **Add to Favorites** (⬚).

The Add a Favorite dialog box appears.

**Note:** You can also display the Add a Favorite dialog box by pressing `Ctrl`+`D`.

④ Edit the page name, as necessary.

⑤ Click **Add**.

## Display a Favourite Web Page

1 Click the **Favorites Center** button ().

2 Click **Favorites**.

The Favorites list appears.

3 Click the Web page you want to display.

The Web page appears.

If you use your Favorites list a lot, you can make it easier to display the pages by keeping the Favorites Center visible.

4 Click the **Pin the Favorites Center** button (). Internet Explorer pins the Favorites Center to the left side of the window.

## Delete a Favourite Web Page

1 Click the **Favorites Center** button ().

2 Click **Favorites**.

3 Right-click the favourite you want to delete.

4 Click **Delete**.

Internet Explorer asks if you are sure you want to delete the favourite.

5 Click **Yes**.

# SEARCH FOR SITES

If you need information on a specific topic, Internet Explorer has a built-in Search feature that enables you to quickly search the Web for sites that have the information you require. You type a word or phrase that represents what you are looking for and Internet Explorer sends the search text to another site that performs the search for you.

The Web has a number of sites called *search engines* that enable you to find what you are looking for. By default, Internet Explorer uses Microsoft's Bing search engine, but you can use other sites.

1. Click in the search box.

2. Type a word, phrase, or question that represents the information you want to find.

3. Click the **Search** button (🔍) or press **Enter**.

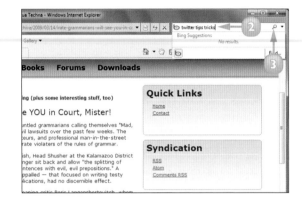

A list of pages that match your search text appears.

4. Click a Web page.

The page appears.

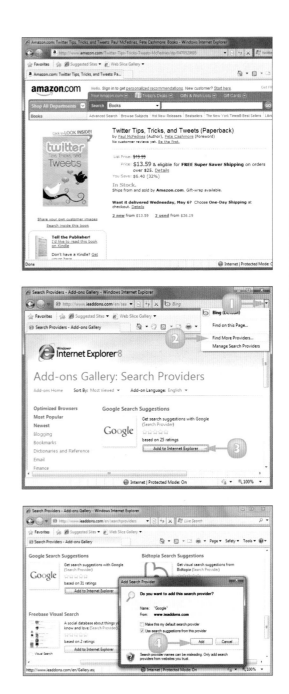

## Use Another Search Engine

 Click the search box ⊡.

② Click **Find More Providers**.

③ Under the search engine you want to use, click **Add to Internet Explorer**.

 Click **Add**.

To use the search engine, click the search box ⊡ and then click the search engine name.

# CONTENTS

# WORKING WITH E-MAIL, CONTACTS, AND EVENTS

You may find that your life is busier than ever and that the number of people you need to stay in touch with, appointments you have to keep, and tasks you have to perform seem to increase daily. Fortunately, you can install the Windows Live Mail program to send e-mail to and read e-mail from friends, family, colleagues, and even total strangers almost anywhere in the world. You can also use Windows Live Mail's Contacts feature to manage your contacts by storing information such as phone numbers, e-mail addresses, street addresses, and much more. Finally, you can use the Calendar feature to enter and track events.

# INSTALL WINDOWS LIVE ESSENTIALS PROGRAMS

Windows Live Mail is not installed on Windows 7 by default. To use the program, you must access the Windows Live Essentials Web site and download and install the program from there.

You can also use the Windows Live Essentials site to install other useful programs that do not come with Windows 7, such as Windows Live Photo Gallery and Windows Live Movie Maker.

 Click **Start**.

② Click the **Getting Started** arrow (▶).

③ Click **Get Windows Live Essentials**.

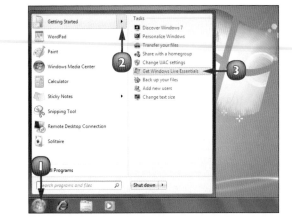

The Windows Live Essentials Web page appears.

④ Click **Download**.

 *All of the programs available on the Windows Live Essentials Web site, including Windows Live Mail, are free. The Windows Live Essentials programs are supplements to Windows 7 but are not included in it as many people prefer to use other programs, such as Microsoft Outlook for e-mail and contacts.*

The File Download - Security
Warning dialog box appears.

 Click **Run**.

**Note:** *If you see the User Account Control
dialog box at this point, provide an
administrator password and click Yes.*

 Click **Close** (⊠) to close
the Windows Live Essentials
Web page.

The Choose the Programs You
Want to Install dialog box
appears.

7 Click the check box beside each
program you want to install
(☐ changes to ☑).

8 Click **Install**.

Windows 7 installs your selected
Windows Live Essentials programs.

✓ *The Windows Live Essentials
installation program adds a
new submenu named Windows
Live to your Start menu. To
launch any Windows Live
Essential program, click Start,
All Programs, and then click
Windows Live. In the submenu
that appears, click the name of
the program you want to run.*

143

# CONFIGURE AN E-MAIL ACCOUNT

Before you can send an e-mail message, you must add your e-mail account to the Windows Live Mail application. This also enables you to use Windows Live Mail to retrieve messages that others have sent to your account.

Your e-mail account is usually a POP (Post Office Protocol) account supplied by your Internet service provider (ISP). The POP account details include your e-mail account login user name and password, and possibly the names of the ISP's incoming and outgoing mail servers.

① Start Windows Live Mail.

The Add an E-mail Account Wizard appears.

② Type your e-mail address.

③ Type your password.

④ Type your name.

⑤ Click **Next**.

**Note:** *If Windows Live Mail tells you it has successfully set up your account, click **Finish** and skip the rest of these steps.*

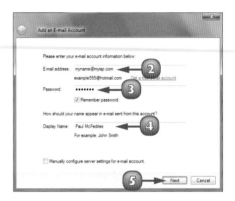

Windows Live Mail prompts you for your e-mail account's server information.

⑥ Type the name of your ISP's incoming mail server.

⑦ Type the e-mail account login user name.

⑧ Type the name of your ISP's outgoing mail server.

⑨ If your ISP uses a different port for outgoing mail, type the port number.

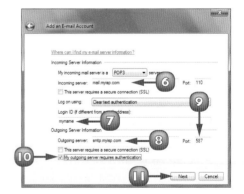

**10** Click this check box if your ISP's outgoing mail server requires authentication (□ changes to ☑).

**11** Click **Next**.

The final wizard dialog box appears.

**12** Click **Finish** at the bottom of dialog box.

Windows Live Mail configures your e-mail account.

**Ⓐ** *Windows Live Mail adds the account to the Folder pane on the left side of the program window.*

**13** To make changes to the account, right-click the account name and then click **Properties**.

**Ⓑ** *In the Properties dialog box that appears, use the tabs to make changes to your settings.*

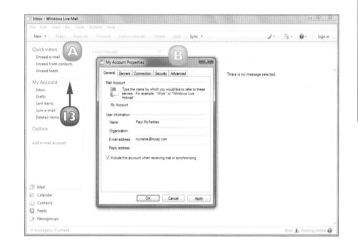

*If you want to configure another e-mail account, click the Add e-mail account link in the Folder pane.*

# SEND AN E-MAIL MESSAGE

If you know the e-mail address of a person or organisation, you can send an e-mail message to that address. In most cases, the message is delivered within a few minutes.

An e-mail address is a set of characters that uniquely identifies the location of an Internet mailbox. Each e-mail address takes the form *username@domain*, where *username* is the name of the person's account with the ISP or within his or her organisation; and *domain* is the Internet name of the company that provides the person's e-mail account. If you do not know any e-mail addresses or if, at first, you prefer to just practice sending messages, you can send messages to your own e-mail address.

 Start Windows Live Mail.

 Click **New**.

**3** Type the e-mail address of the recipient.

> **A** *To send the message to another person, click **Show Cc & Bcc** and type an e-mail address in the **Cc** field.*

**4** Type a title for the message.

**5** Type the message.

> **B** *Use the buttons in the Formatting bar to format the message text.*

 Click **Send**.

Windows Live Mail sends your message.

**Note:** *Windows Live Mail stores a copy of your message in the Sent Items folder.*

STOP **Press Alt, click Format, and then click Plain text ( appears beside the command) to send an email without formatting.**

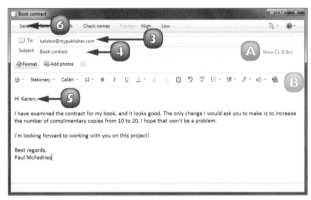

# ADD SOMEONE TO YOUR CONTACTS

You can use Windows Live Contacts to store the names and e-mail addresses of people with whom you frequently correspond. You do that by creating a new contact, which stores data about a person or company. For example, you can store a person's name, company name, phone numbers, e-mail address and instant messaging data, street address, notes, and much more.

When you choose a name from Windows Live Contacts while composing a message, Windows Live Mail automatically adds the contact's e-mail address. This is faster and more accurate than typing the address by hand.

 In Windows Live Mail, click
**Contacts** ().

**Note:** *You can also open Windows Live Contacts by pressing* **Ctrl**+**Shift**+**C**.

The Windows Live Contacts window appears.

 Click **New**.

The Add a Contact dialog box appears.

 Type the person's first name.

 Type the person's last name.

 Type the person's e-mail address.

**A** *You can use the other tabs to store more information about the contact, including home and business addresses and phone numbers, spouse name, birthday, and more.*

 Click **Add contact**.

Windows Live Contacts adds the person to the Contacts list.

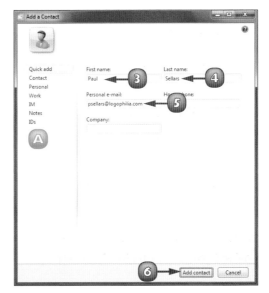

# SELECT A CONTACT ADDRESS

After you have some e-mail addresses and names in your Windows Live Contacts list, you can select the address you want directly from Windows Live Contacts, when composing a message, instead of typing the address. This is much faster and more accurate than typing the address by hand, particularly if you are sending the message to multiple people.

 In Windows Live Mail, click **New** to start a new message.

 Click **To**.

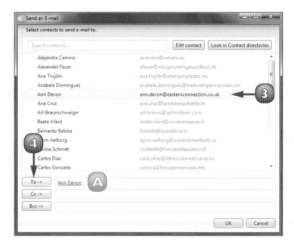

The Send an E-mail dialog box appears.

 Click the person to whom you want to send the message.

 Click **To**.

(A) *The person's name appears in the To box.*

**Note:** *You can also double-click a contact to add that person to the To field.*

(5) Repeat Steps **3** and **4** to add other recipients to the To box.

**6** To send a copy of the message to a recipient, click the person's name.

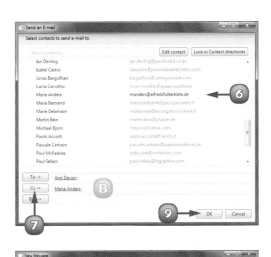

**7** Click **Cc**.

**B** *The person's name appears in the message recipients box.*

**8** Repeat Steps **6** and **7** to add other recipients to the Cc box.

**9** Click **OK**.

**C** *Windows Live Mail adds the recipients to the To and Cc lines of the new message.*

 **In Windows Live Contacts, click the name of the person to whom you want to send a message and then click the E-mail button in the toolbar. The contact's name is automatically added to the To field of a new message.**

**Bcc stands for blind courtesy copy. Addresses in the Bcc field are not displayed to the other message recipients. If you do not want Windows Live Mail to display the Bcc field in the message window, click Hide Cc & Bcc.**

# ADD A FILE ATTACHMENT

You might find that you need to send someone something more complex than a simple text e-mail, such as budget numbers, a slide show, or some form of media that you want to share, such as an image or a song. Because these more complex types of data usually come in a separate file – such as a spreadsheet, a presentation file, a picture file, or a music file – it makes sense to send that file to your recipient. You do this by attaching the file to an e-mail message. The other person can open the document after he or she receives your message.

## Add an Attachment from a Dialog Box

**1** Click **New** to start a new message.

**2** Click **Attach**.

The Open dialog box appears.

**3** Click the file you want to attach.

**4** Click **Open**.

**A** *Windows Live Mail attaches the file to the message.*

**5** Repeat Steps **2** to **4** to attach additional files to the message.

## Add an Attachment Directly

**1** Open the folder that contains the file you want to send as an attachment.

**2** Click the file.

**3** Click **E-mail**.

Windows Live Mail creates a new message and attaches the file.

**STOP** *There is no practical limit to the number of files you can attach to a message. However, you should be careful with the total size of the files you send. Many Internet service providers (ISPs) place a limit on the size of a message's attachments, which is usually between 2MB and 10MB. In general, use e-mail to send only a few small files at a time.*

# ADD A SIGNATURE

In an e-mail message, a *signature* is a small amount of text that appears at the bottom of the message. Instead of typing this information manually, you can create the signature once and then have Windows Live Mail add the signature automatically to any message you send.

Signatures usually contain personal contact information, such as your phone numbers, business address, and e-mail and Web site addresses. Some people supplement their signatures with wise or witty quotations. Windows Live Mail supports multiple signatures, which is useful if you use Mail for different purposes such as business and personal e-mail. You can configure Windows Live Mail to automatically add one of your signatures to any message you send.

**1** Click **Menus** ().

**2** Click **Options**.

The Options dialog box appears.

**3** Click the **Signatures** tab.

**4** Click **New**.

**A** *Windows Live Mail creates a new signature.*

**5** Type the signature text.

**6** Click **Rename**.

**7** Type a name for the signature and press Enter.

**8** Click **OK**.

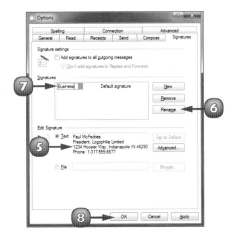

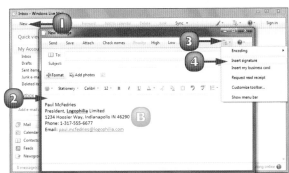

## Insert a Signature Manually

 Click **New** to start a new message.

**2** In the message text area, move the insertion point to the location where you want the signature to appear.

**3** Click **Menus** (🗐).

**4** Click **Insert signature**.

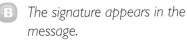

**Note:** *If you have more than one signature, click the one you want to use from the menu that appears.*

**B** *The signature appears in the message.*

 *Windows Live Mail can add a signature automatically to the bottom of every new message. Follow Steps 1 to 3 to display the Signatures tab. Click Add signatures to all outgoing messages ( changes to ).*

153

# RECEIVE AND READ E-MAIL MESSAGES

You must connect to your mail provider's incoming mail server to retrieve and read messages sent to you.

When another person sends you an e-mail message, that message ends up in your e-mail account's mailbox on the incoming mail server your ISP or e-mail provider maintains. However, that company does not automatically pass along that message to you. Instead, you must use Mail to connect to your mailbox on the incoming mail server and retrieve any messages waiting for you. By default, Windows Live Mail checks for new messages automatically when you start the program and then every 30 minutes while you are online.

## Receive E-mail Messages

1. Click **Inbox**.

2. Click **Sync**.

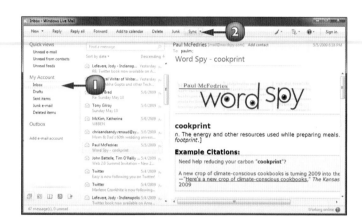

A. *If you have new messages, they appear in your Inbox folder in bold type.*

B. *This symbol (⬚) means that the message has a file attached.*

C. *This symbol (⬇) means the message was sent as low priority.*

D. *This symbol (❗) means the message was sent as high priority.*

## Read a Message

 Click the message.

② Read the message text in the preview pane.

**Note:** *If you want to open the message in its own window, double-click the message.*

## Change how often Windows Live Mail Checks for Messages

① Click **Menus** (🔳) and then click **Options**.

② In the Options dialog box, click the **General** tab.

③ If you do not want Windows Live Mail to check for messages when the program starts, click **Send and receive messages at startup** (☑ changes to ☐).

④ Type a new time interval, in minutes, that you want Windows Live Mail to use when automatically checking for new messages.

⑤ Click **OK**.

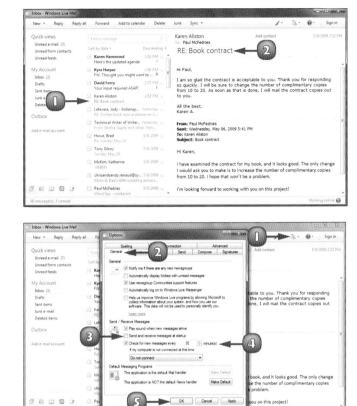

# REPLY TO A MESSAGE

When a message you receive requires some kind of response – whether it is answering a question, supplying information, or providing comments or criticisms – you can reply to it.

Most replies go only to the person who sent the original message. However, it is also possible to send the reply to all the people who were included in the original message's To line and Cc lines.

 Click the message to which you want to reply.

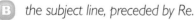 Click the reply type you want to use:

**Reply** responds only to the first address on the From line.

**Reply All** responds to all the addresses in the From and Cc lines.

A message window appears. Windows Live Mail inserts:

Ⓐ *the recipient addresses.*

Ⓑ *the subject line, preceded by Re.*

Ⓒ *the original message information.*

③ Edit the original message to include only the relevant text.

④ Click the area above the original message text and type your reply.

⑤ Click **Send**.

Windows Live Mail sends your reply and stores a copy of it in the Sent Items folder.

# FORWARD A MESSAGE

If a message has information relevant to another person, you can forward a copy of that message to the other person. You can also include your own comments in the forward.

When it creates the forward message, Windows Live Mail automatically adds "Fw:" to the beginning of the subject line to indicate the message is a forward.

① Click the message that you want to forward.

② Click **Forward**.

In the message window Windows Live Mail automatically inserts:

Ⓐ the subject line, preceded by Fw.

Ⓑ the original message's information at the bottom of the message.

③ Type the e-mail address of the person to whom you are forwarding the message.

④ Edit the original message to include only the text relevant to your forward.

⑤ Click the area above the original message text and type your comments.

⑥ Click **Send**.

Windows Live Mail sends your forward.

**Note:** *Windows Live Mail stores a copy of your sent message in the Sent Items folder.*

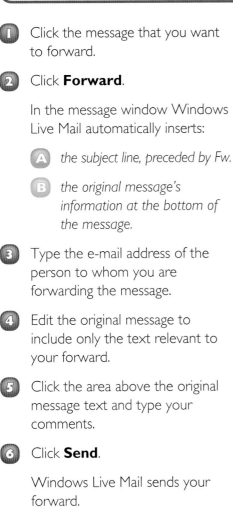

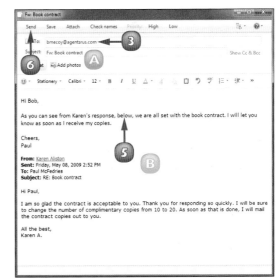

# OPEN AND SAVE AN ATTACHMENT

If you receive an e-mail message that has a file attached, you can open the attachment to view the contents of the file. You can also save the attachment as a file on your computer.

Be careful when dealing with attached files. Computer viruses are often transmitted by e-mail attachments. If you do not know the person who sent you the file, do not open it. If the message came from someone you know and you were expecting the file, then it should be safe to open the file; if you were not expecting the file, however, you should write back to have the person confirm that the file is legitimate.

## Open An Attachment

 Click the message that has the attachment, as indicated by the **Attachment** symbol (⬚).

A list of the message attachments appears.

② Double-click the attachment you want to open.

Windows Live Mail asks you to confirm that you want to open the file.

③ Click **Open**.

The file opens in the appropriate program.

 *Windows 7 may display a dialog box saying that the file "does not have a program associated with it." If you are not sure what program you need, ask the person who sent you the file.*

## Save An Attachment

 Click the message that has the attachment, as indicated by the Attachment symbol (▥).

A list of the message attachments appears.

 Right-click the attachment you want to save.

**3** Click **Save as**.

The Save Attachment As dialog box appears.

**4** Use the File Name text box to edit the file name, if desired.

**5** Select the folder into which you want the file saved.

**6** Click **Save**.

**STOP** *If you cannot click the Save As command, Windows Live Mail has determined that the attached file may be unsafe, meaning that it may harbour a virus or other malicious code. If you are certain the file is safe, click Menus (▤), Safety*

*Options, the Security tab, and then Do not allow attachments to be saved or opened that could potentially be a virus (☑ changes to ☐). Be sure to reactivate this feature after you have opened or saved the attachment.*

# SWITCH TO CALENDAR

With Calendar, the scheduling program that comes with Windows Live Mail, you can create and work with events, which are either scheduled appointments such as meetings, lunches, and visits to the dentist, or all-day activities, such as conferences or vacations. The Calendar feature also enables you to create recurring events that automatically repeat at the interval you specify. To get started, you must first switch to the Calendar feature.

① Click **Calendar** (▣).

**Note:** You can also open the Calendar by pressing Ctrl + Shift + X.

The Calendar window appears.

② When you finish your scheduling chores, click the **Mail** button (▣) or press Ctrl + Shift + J to return to the Mail feature.

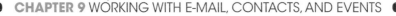

160

# UNDERSTANDING THE CALENDAR

Windows Live Mail's Calendar makes scheduling easy. However, you can make it even easier by taking some time now to learn the layout of the Calendar window. The most important features are the Date Navigator, the current date display, the event list, and the Calendars list.

 **Date Navigator**

This area shows the current month, and you use the Date Navigator to select the date on which you want to schedule an event, all-day event, or task. See the "Navigate the Calendar" section, later in this chapter, to learn how to use the Date Navigator.

**B Current Date**

This area shows the date that is currently selected in the Date Navigator.

**C Event List**

This area shows the events that you have scheduled. In Day view, as shown here, the event list is divided into half-hour increments.

**D Calendars**

This area shows a list of your calendars. You get a single calendar to start with, but you can add more calendars as described in the "Add a Calendar" section, later in this chapter.

# NAVIGATE THE CALENDAR

You use the Date Navigator to display dates in the Calendar and you can navigate dates by month or by year.

You can also change the calendar view to suit your needs. For example, you can show a single day's appointments if you want to concentrate on that day's activities. Similarly, you can view a week's appointments if you want to get a larger sense of what your schedule looks like.

**①** Click the **Next Month** button (▶) until the month of your event appears.

**②** If you go too far, click the **Previous Month** button (◀) to move back.

**③** Click a date.

**Ⓐ** The date appears in the events list.

**④** If you want to return to today's date, click **Go to today**.

**⑤** In the Date Navigator, click the month.

Calendar switches to Year view.

**⑥** Click the **Next Year** (▶) and **Previous Year** (◀) buttons until the year you want appears.

**Ⓐ** To see the day, week or month that includes the date selected click **Day**, **Week** or **Month**.

**⑦** Click the month when your event occurs.

Calendar switches to Month view.

# CREATE AN EVENT

You can help organise your life by using Windows Live Mail's Calendar to record your events.

If the event has a set time and duration – for example, a meeting or a lunch date – you add the event directly to the calendar as a regular appointment. If the event has no set time – for example, a birthday, anniversary, or multiple-day event such as a sales meeting or vacation – you can create an all-day event. If you have an activity or appointment that recurs at regular intervals, you can create an event and configure it to automatically repeat in Calendar.

 Navigate to the date when the event occurs.

 Click the time when the event starts.

**Note:** *If the event is more than half an hour, you can also click and drag the mouse ⌕ over the full event period.*

 Click **New**.

**Note:** *You can also press* Ctrl + Shift + E.

Calendar displays the New Event dialog box.

4 Type a name for the event.

5 Enter the event location.

6 If the event lasts all day, click **All day** (☐ changes to ☑).

7 Enter the correct Start time.

8 Enter the correct End time.

9 Type notes related to the event.

10 Click **Save & close**.

Calendar adds the event to the list.

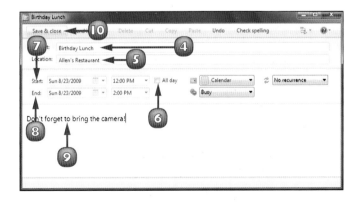

# ADD A CALENDAR

If you have different schedules that you want to keep separate, you can add another calendar. For example, you might want to have one calendar for work events and a second calendar for personal events. You could also set up different calendars for individual people, different projects, separate clients, and so on.

You can assign different colours to each calendar, which helps you to see at a glance which event belongs to which calendar.

① Click **Add calendar**.

**Note:** Another way to start a new calendar is to press Ctrl + Shift + D.

The Add a Calendar dialog box appears.

② Type a name for the calendar.

③ Click the colour you want to use for the calendar.

**4** Type an optional description for the calendar.

**5** If you want Windows Live Mail to use this calendar as the default for new events, click **Make this my primary calendar** (☐ changes to ☑).

**6** Click **Save**.

**A** *The new calendar appears in the Calendars list.*

---

☑ **Click the calendar you want to use and then click New event to create an event in a specific calendar. In the New Event window, click the Calendar ⊡ and then click the calendar you want to use. For an existing event, double-click the event, click the Calendar ⊡, and then click the calendar.**

☑ **The default name of "Calendar" is not very descriptive, so it is a good idea to rename it to something more useful. In the Calendars list, click Calendar and then click Properties. Use the Calendar name text box to type a new name, and then click Save.**

# CONTENTS

# IMPLEMENTING SECURITY IN WINDOWS 7

Threats to your computer-related security and privacy often come from the Internet in the form of system intruders, such as junk e-mail, viruses, and identity thieves. However, many security and privacy violations occur right at your computer by someone simply using your computer while you are not around. To protect yourself and your family, you need to understand these threats and know what you can do to thwart them.

This chapter gives you some background information about security in Windows 7 and shows you various methods for securing your computer.

# UNDERSTANDING WINDOWS 7 SECURITY

Before getting to the details of securing your PC, it helps to take a step back and look at the security and privacy tools that Windows 7 makes available.

These tools include your user account password, Windows 7's User Account Control and Parental Controls features, the Windows Firewall and Windows Defender programs, and the anti-phishing and anti-spam features of Internet Explorer and Windows Live Mail.

## User Account Password

Windows 7 security begins with assigning a password to each user account on the computer. This prevents unauthorised users from accessing the system and it enables you to lock your computer. See "Protect an Account with a Password" and "Lock Your Computer," later in this chapter.

## User Account Control

User Account Control asks you to confirm certain actions that could conceivably harm your system. If you have an administrator account, you click **Yes** to continue; if you have a standard account, you must enter an administrator's user name and password to continue.

## Parental Controls

If one or more children use your computer, you can use Windows 7's Parental Controls to protect those children from inadvertently running certain programs, playing unsuitable games, and using the computer at inappropriate times.

## Windows Firewall

Because when your computer is connected to the Internet, it is possible for another person on the Internet to access your computer and infect it with a virus or cause other damage, Windows 7 comes with the Windows Firewall feature turned on. This prevents intruders from accessing your computer while you are online.

## Windows Defender

*Spyware* is a software program that installs on your computer without your knowledge or consent. This program surreptitiously gathers data from your computer, steals your passwords, displays advertisements, and hijacks your Web browser. To prevent spyware from installing on your computer, Windows 7 includes the Windows Defender program.

## Phishing

*Phishing* refers to e-mail messages or Web sites that appear to come from legitimate businesses and organisations but actually come from a scam artist. The purpose of the message or site is to fool you into divulging personal or private data, such as passwords and credit card numbers. Internet Explorer and Windows Live Mail come with anti-phishing features to help prevent this.

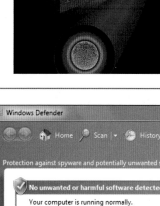

## Junk E-mail

Junk e-mail – or *spam* – refers to unsolicited, commercial e-mail messages that advertise anything from baldness cures to cheap printer cartridges. Many spams advertise deals that are simply fraudulent and others feature such unsavoury practices as linking to adult-oriented sites or sites that install spyware. Windows Live Mail comes with a junk e-mail filter; see "Set the Junk E-mail Protection Level," later in this chapter.

# CHECK ACTION CENTER FOR SECURITY PROBLEMS

In Windows 7, the new Action Center displays messages about the current state of your PC. In particular, Action Center warns you if your computer has any current security problems.

For example, the Action Center tells you if your PC does not have virus protection installed, or if the Windows Defender spyware database is out of date or turned off. Action Center also warns you if User Account Control is turned off or if the Windows Firewall is deactivated.

① Click **Start**.

② Click **Control Panel**.

The Control Panel window appears.

③ Click **Review your computer's status**.

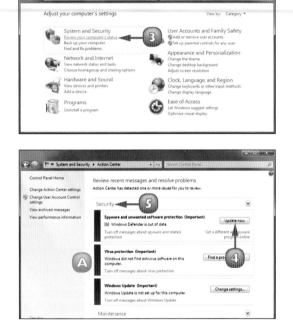

The Action Center window appears.

Ⓐ Review the messages in the Security section.

④ Click a message button to resolve the security issue, such as clicking **Update now** if Windows Defender is out of date.

⑤ Click **Security**.

**6** Scroll down the Action Center window.

Action Center displays a summary of all your system's security settings.

## See Action Center Messages

**1** Click the **Action Center** icon () in the taskbar's notification area.

The current Action Center messages appear in the popup.

**2** To launch Action Center, click **Open Action Center**.

# PROTECT AN ACCOUNT WITH A PASSWORD

You can protect your Windows 7 user account with a password. This is a good idea because otherwise another user can log on to your account just by clicking your user name in the Welcome screen. Once you have a password associated with your user account, another user can still click your user name in the Welcome screen, but that person must then enter your password before Windows 7 goes any further.

For maximum security, make sure you create a strong password that cannot be easily guessed or hacked. See the tip on the next page.

① Click **Start**.

② Click **Control Panel**.

The Control Panel window appears.

③ Click **Add or remove user accounts**.

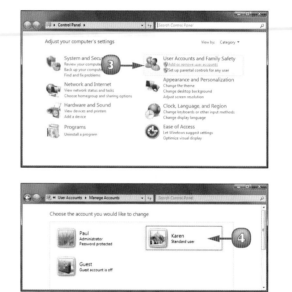

The Manage Accounts window appears.

④ Click the user account you want to work with.

172

The Change an Account window appears.

 **5** Click **Create a password**.

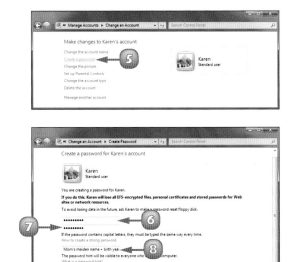

The Create Password window appears.

 **6** Type the password.

 **7** Type the password again.

**8** Type a word or phrase to use as a password hint in case you forget the password.

**9** Click **Create password**.

Windows 7 adds the password to the user account.

---

*Do not use obvious items such as your name or a word such as "password." Your password should be at least eight characters long and it should include at least one character from each of the following three sets: lowercase letters, uppercase letters, and numbers.*

*To change the password, follow Steps 1 to 4 to open the Change an Account window. Click the Change the password link to open the Change Password dialog box. Type your existing password, follow Steps 6 to 8 to specify the new password and hint, and then click Change password.*

# LOCK YOUR COMPUTER

Protecting your account with a password prevents someone from logging on to your account, but what happens when you leave your desk? If you remain logged on to the system, any person who sits down at your computer can use it to view and change files. To prevent this, lock your computer, which hides your desktop and displays the Windows 7 Welcome screen.

Once your computer is locked, anyone who tries to use your computer will first have to enter your password in the Welcome screen.

**①** Click **Start**.

**②** Click the power button arrow (▶).

**③** Click **Lock**.

Windows 7 locks your computer.

The word "Locked" appears under your user name.

## Unlock Your Computer

 Click inside the password text box.

 Type your password.

 Click **Go** ().

Windows 7 unlocks your computer and restores your desktop.

## Make it Easier to Lock your Computer

 Right-click **Start** and then click **Properties**.

The Taskbar and Start Menu Properties dialog box appears.

 Click the **Power button action** ⊡ and then click **Lock**.

 Click **OK**.

Windows 7 customises the Start menu's Power button to lock your computer instead of shutting it down.

 *You can also press* ⊞+🄛 *to access the lock command directly.*

175

# SET THE JUNK E-MAIL PROTECTION LEVEL

You can make junk messages easier to manage by setting the Windows Live Mail junk e-mail protection level. You can set a higher level if you receive many junk messages each day and a lower level if you receive very few junk messages.

The higher the protection level, the more aggressively Windows Live Mail checks for junk e-mail. All suspected junk messages get moved to the Junk E-mail folder. If a legitimate message is moved to Junk E-mail by accident, you can mark the message as not junk.

① In Windows Live Mail, click **Menus** (▣).

② Click **Safety options**.

The Safety Options dialog box appears.

③ Click the **Options** tab.

Click the protection level you want (◎ changes to ◉):

 Click **No Automatic Filtering** if you receive very few junk messages each day.

**B** Click **Low** if you receive a moderate number of junk messages.

**C** Click **High** if you receive many junk messages each day.

**5** Click **OK**.

Windows Live Mail puts the new protection level into effect.

## Mark a Message as Not Junk

**1** Click the Junk E-mail folder.

 Click the message.

 Click **Not junk**.

Windows Mail returns the message to the Inbox folder.

177

# CONTENTS

# CUSTOMISING WINDOWS 7

Windows 7 comes with a number of features that enable you to personalise your computer. For example, you can change the appearance of Windows 7 to suit your taste, including selecting a new desktop background, choosing a screen saver, and changing the Windows 7 colour scheme.

You can also change the way Windows 7 works to make it easier to use and more efficient. For example, you can change the icons that appear on the Start menu and you can configure the taskbar.

# OPEN THE PERSONALIZATION WINDOW

To make changes to many of Windows 7's display options, you need to know how to open the Personalization window.

The Personalization window is one of the most powerful and useful features of Windows 7. With the Personalization window you can change the desktop background, select a new colour scheme, set up a screen saver, and more. With the Personalization window you can also apply themes to quickly and easily change the overall look of Windows 7.

**1** Click **Start**.

**2** Click **Control Panel**.

The Control Panel window appears.

**3** Click **Appearance and Personalization**.

The Appearance and Personalization window appears.

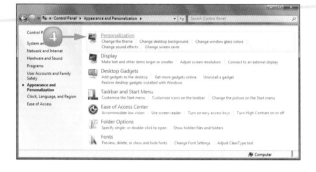

**4** Click **Personalization**.

The Personalization window appears.

**Note:** *A quicker way to open the Personalization window is to right-click an empty section of the desktop and then click Personalize.*

**5** Scroll down to view the available themes and click one to change the desktop background, screen saver, and colour scheme all at once.

**Note:** *Each theme also includes its own set of desktop icons, sound effects, and mouse pointers.*

**6** Click the **Close** button (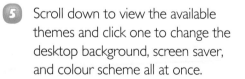) when you are finished working with this window.

# CHANGE THE DESKTOP BACKGROUND

For a different look, you can change the desktop background to display a different image or a specific colour.

Windows 7 comes with more than three dozen desktop background images, which include scenes of nature, architectural photos, fantasy characters, and more. If none of the built-in desktop backgrounds appeal to you, you can use one of your own photos as the background.

① Open the Personalization window.

② Click **Desktop Background**.

The Desktop Background window appears.

③ Click the **Picture location** ⊡ and then click the background gallery you want to use.

**Note:** *If you would prefer to use your own image, click Pictures Library. You can also click Browse and select a file.*

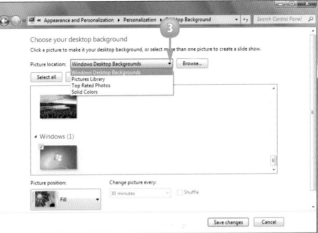

Windows 7 displays the backgrounds in the selected gallery.

④ Click **Clear all**.

⑤ Click the image or colour you want to use.

⑥ Click the **Picture position** ⊡ and then click the positioning you want.

⑦ Click **Save changes**.

⑧ Click the **Close** button (⊠).

The picture or colour you selected appears on the desktop.

# SET THE SCREEN SAVER

If you leave your monitor on for long stretches while your computer is idle, the image can end up temporarily "burned" into the monitor's screen. A screen saver prevents this by displaying a moving image.

However, the temporarily burned image will not damage your monitor over the long term, so many people set up a screen saver to have something interesting to look at while their computer is idle.

1 Open the Personalization window.

2 Click **Screen Saver**.

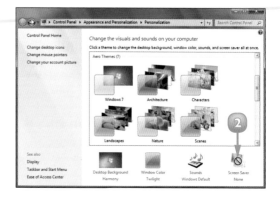

The Screen Saver Settings dialog box appears.

3 Click the **Screen saver** ☑ and then click the screen saver you want to use.

Ⓐ A preview of the screen saver appears.

**Note:** Not all screen savers can display the small preview. To see an actual preview, click Preview. When you are done, move the mouse ▷ or press a key to stop the preview.

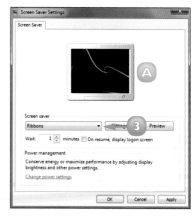

182

182

182

CHAPTER 11 CUSTOMISING WINDOWS 7

**4** Click the **Wait** ⊞ to specify the number of minutes of computer idle time after which the screen saver appears.

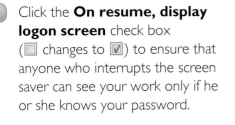

**5** Click the **On resume, display logon screen** check box (☐ changes to ☑) to ensure that anyone who interrupts the screen saver can see your work only if he or she knows your password.

**6** Click **OK**.

The screen saver appears after your computer is idle for the number of minutes you specified in Step **4**.

*Note: To interrupt the screen saver, move the mouse ⍐ or press* **Shift** *on the keyboard.*

183

# CHANGE THE WINDOWS 7 COLOUR SCHEME

You can personalise your copy of Windows 7 by choosing a different colour scheme, which Windows 7 applies to the window borders, taskbar, and Start menu.

You can also customise the Windows 7 look by toggling the transparent glass effect on and off and by setting the colour intensity. Windows 7 enables you to create your own colours, each of which is a combination of three properties: hue (the colour), saturation (the purity of the colour), and brightness (how much grey is mixed in with the colour).

1 Open the Personalization window.

2 Click **Window Color**.

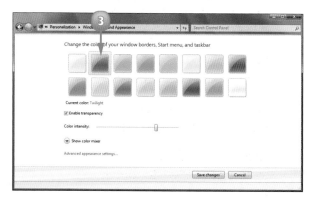

The Window Color and Appearance window appears.

**Note:** *If you see the Window Color and Appearance dialog box, instead, see the next page.*

3 Click the colour you want to use.

Windows 7 changes the colour of the window border.

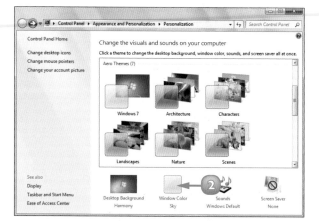

**④** If you do not want to see the glass effect, click **Enable transparency** (☑ changes to ☐).

**⑤** Click and drag the **Color intensity** slider to set the colour intensity.

**⑥** Click **Show color mixer** (the prompt changes to Hide color mixer).

**⑦** Click and drag the **Hue**, **Saturation**, and **Brightness** sliders to set your custom colour.

**⑧** Click **Save changes**.

Windows 7 applies the new colour scheme.

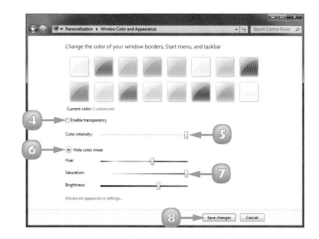

## Use the Window Color and Appearance Dialog Box

On systems with lower-end graphics cards or little graphics memory, you change the colour scheme in this dialog.

**①** Click the Item ▾ and click the object you want to customise.

**②** Click ▾ in each Color list and select colours for the object.

**③** Use the Font, Size, Color, Bold, and Italics controls to format any text.

**④** Repeat Steps **1** to **3** to customise other items.

**⑤** Click **OK**.

# CUSTOMISE THE START MENU

You can personalise how the Start menu looks and operates to suit your style and the way you work. For example, you can turn off the lists of recently used documents and programs for privacy.

You can also control the items that appear on the right side of the menu. For example, you can add and remove items, and you can change whether some items appear as links or menus.

You can also customise the number of recent programs that appear on the Start menu and the number of items that appear in jump lists.

1. Right-click **Start**.

2. Click **Properties**.

The Taskbar and Start Menu Properties dialog box appears with the Start Menu tab displayed.

3. If you do not want Windows 7 to list your recently used programs, click here (☑ changes to ☐).

4. If you do not want Windows 7 to list your recently used documents, click here (☑ changes to ☐).

5. Click **Customize**.

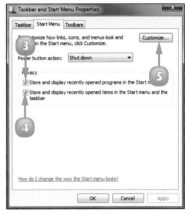

The Customize Start Menu dialog box appears.

**(A)** *Use the Start menu items list to control the icons that appear on the Start menu.*

**(B)** *Some items have several option buttons that control how they appear on the Start menu; click the option you want ( ⊙ changes to ⦿ ).*

**(C)** *Some items have check boxes that determine whether the item appears ( ☑ ) or does not appear ( ☐ ) on the Start menu.*

**6** Click ⊞ to change the maximum number of your recent programs that can appear on the Start menu.

**7** Click ⊞ to change the maximum number of the recent items that can appear in jump lists.

**8** Click **OK** to return to the Taskbar and Start Menu Properties dialog box.

**9** Click **OK**.

Windows 7 puts your new Start menu settings into effect.

**You can remove a program from the Start menu's list of most often used programs. Click Start, right-click the program and click Remove from this list.**

**You can add a program permanently to the Start menu. Click Start and then right-click the program. In the shortcut menu, click Pin to Start Menu. The program's icon now appears in the top part of the menu.**

# CUSTOMISE THE TASKBAR

You can personalise how the taskbar operates and looks to make it more efficient and suited to your working style.

For example, you can unlock the taskbar, which enables you to change its size. You can temporarily hide the taskbar to give your programs more room on the desktop or change the taskbar location. You can display smaller taskbar icons, which enables you to fit more icons on the taskbar. You can also group taskbar buttons from the same application, which gives you more room to display other taskbar icons. Finally, you can customise the notification area icons.

① Right-click an empty section of the taskbar.

② Click **Properties**.

The Taskbar and Start Menu Properties dialog box appears with the Taskbar tab displayed.

③ Click **Lock the taskbar** (☑ changes to ☐) to unlock and resize the taskbar.

④ Click **Auto-hide the taskbar** (☐ changes to ☑) to hide the taskbar.

**Note:** *To display the hidden taskbar, move the mouse ↳ to the bottom of the screen.*

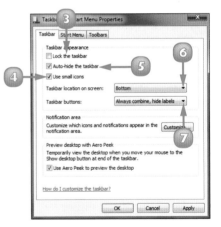

⑤ Click **Use small icons** (☐ changes to ☑) to fit more icons on the taskbar.

⑥ Click the **Taskbar location on screen** ⊡ and then click the location you prefer.

⑦ Click the **Taskbar buttons** ⊡ and then click the grouping option you prefer.

188

## Customise the Notification Area

 Click **Customize**.

The Notification Area Icons window appears.

**2** For each notification area icon, click ⏷ and then click the setting you prefer.

**3** If you choose to hide one or more notification area icons, you can click here to display the hidden icons.

**4** Click this link to turn the system icons on or off.

**5** Click **OK** to return to the taskbar properties.

**6** Click **OK**.

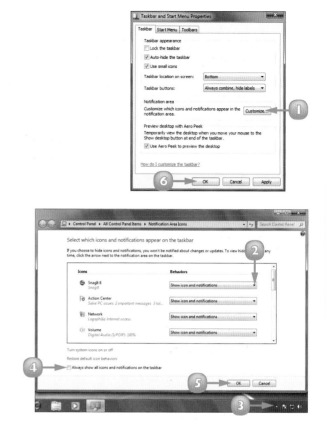

*You can group taskbar buttons so that a single button shows for a program that has multiple windows open. To switch to one of those windows, click the taskbar button and then click the window name.*

*The notification area icon options control whether the icon appears in the notification area and whether you see messages from the icon's program. Choose **Show icon and notifications** to see both the icon and its messages; choose **Only show notifications** to hide the icon but still see the messages; or choose **Hide icons and notifications** to see neither the icon nor the messages.*

# CONTENTS

## MAINTAINING WINDOWS 7

To keep your system running smoothly, maintain top performance, and reduce the risk of computer problems, you need to perform some routine maintenance chores. This chapter shows you the most important of those chores, with an emphasis on maintaining your hard drive. For example, you learn how to monitor your hard drive's available space and defragment your hard drive for better performance.

You also learn how to back up your files and how to restore files from your backups.

# CHECK HARD DRIVE FREE SPACE

You can check how much free space your hard drive has. This is important because if you run out of room on your hard drive, you cannot install more programs or create more documents.

Of particular concern is the hard drive on which Windows 7 is installed, usually drive C. If this hard drive's free space gets low – say, less than 20 percent of the total hard drive space – Windows 7 runs slowly and may also experience problems, such as freezing.

 Click **Start**.

 Click **Computer**.

**Note:** You can also check the free space on CDs, DVDs, memory cards, or flash drives. Before you continue, insert the disc, card, or drive.

The Computer window appears.

 Click the **View** icon ⊡.

 Click **Tiles**.

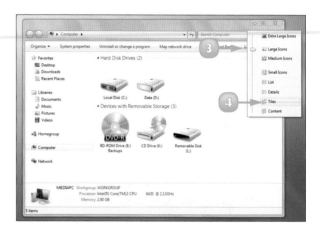

Information about the drive appears with the drive icon.

Ⓐ The amount of free space.

Ⓑ The total amount of space.

The bar gives you a visual indication of how much disk space is used on the drive:

Ⓒ It is blue when a drive has sufficient disk space.

Ⓓ It turns red when a drive's disk space is low.

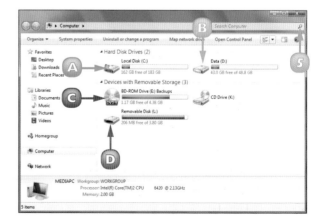

 Click the **Close** button (❌) to close the Computer window.

## Increase Hard Drive Space

1. Delete Documents. If you have documents — particularly images, music, and videos — that you no longer need, delete them.

2. Remove Programs. If you have programs that you no longer use, uninstall them (see "Uninstall a Program" in Chapter 2).

3. Use the Disk Cleanup program to delete files that Windows 7 no longer uses. Click **Start**, **All Programs**.

4. Click **Accessories**.

5. Click **System Tools**.

6. Click **Disk Cleanup**.

7. If the Drive Selection dialog box appears, click the **Drives** ⊡ and then click the hard drive you want to clean up.

8. Click **OK**.

   The Disk Cleanup dialog box appears.

   Ⓐ This area displays the total amount of drive space you can free up.

   Ⓑ This area displays the amount of drive space the activated options will free up.

9. Click the check box (☐ changes to ☑) for each file type that you want to delete.

10. Click **OK**.

# DEFRAGMENT YOUR HARD DRIVE ON A SCHEDULE

You can make Windows 7, and your programs, run faster, and your documents open more quickly, by defragmenting your hard drive on a regular schedule.

Most files are stored on your computer in several pieces, and over time, those pieces often get scattered around your hard drive, which means your hard drive becomes fragmented. This slows down your computer because Windows 7 has to spend extra time locating and opening each piece of a file. Defragmenting improves performance by bringing all those pieces together, making finding and opening each file faster.

① Click **Start**.

② Click **All Programs**.

**Note:** When you click **All Programs**, the command name changes to Back.

③ Click **Accessories**.

④ Click **System Tools**.

⑤ Click **Disk Defragmenter**.

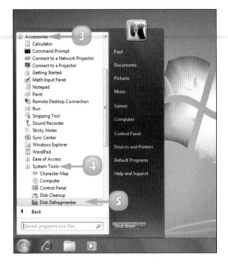

The Disk Defragmenter window appears.

⑥ Click **Configure schedule**.

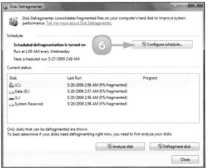

The Disk Defragmenter: Modify Schedule dialog box appears.

**7** Click **Run on a schedule (recommended)** (☐ changes to ☑).

**8** Click the **Frequency** and then click the frequency with which you want to defragment (Daily, Weekly, or Monthly).

**9** Click the **Day** and click either the day of the week (for a Weekly schedule) or the day of the month (for a Monthly schedule).

**10** Click the **Time** and then click the time of day to run the defragment.

**11** Click **OK**.

**A** *The new schedule appears here.*

**12** If you want to defragment your drives now, click **Defragment disk**.

**13** Click **Close**.

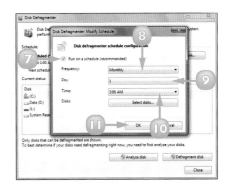

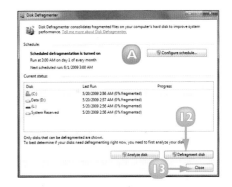

 *If you use your computer every day, you should defragment your hard drive weekly. If you use your computer only occasionally, you should defragment your hard drive monthly.*

 *Allow at least 15 minutes for the defragmentation and know that it could take more than an hour.*

# BACK UP FILES

You can use the Windows Backup program to make backup copies of your important files. If a system problem causes you to lose one or more files, you can restore them from the backup.

To set up Windows 7 for backups, you run through a short configuration procedure. Once that is done, you do not have to worry about backups again because Windows 7 handles everything for you automatically. In the Windows Backup program, you can back up to a recordable CD or DVD drive, to another hard drive on your system, or to a network location.

① Click **Start**.

② Click **All Programs**.

**Note:** When you click **All Programs**, the command name changes to Back.

③ Click **Maintenance**.

④ Click **Backup and Restore**.

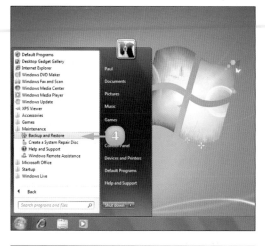

The Backup and Restore window appears.

⑤ Click **Set up backup**.

The Set Up Backup dialog box appears.

⑥ Click the drive where you want to store the backup.

⑦ For a network backup, click **Save on a network**, click **Browse**, click the network folder, and then click **OK**.

⑧ Click **Next**.

The What Do You Want to Back Up? dialog box appears.

⑨ Click **Let Windows choose (recommended)** (◎ changes to ◉).

Ⓐ If you want to specify what to include in the backup, click **Let me choose** (◎ changes to ◉), instead, and then make your selections in the next dialog box.

⑩ Click **Next**.

✓ **A system image is an exact copy of your entire system. If your computer crashes and will no longer start, you can use a system image backup to restore the entire system. If you back up to another hard drive or a network drive, a system image is automatically included in the backup.**

✓ **After you have configured your initial backup, Windows Backup runs automatically once a week, although you can change that schedule if you prefer to back up more or less often.**

continued ➡

197

By default, Windows Backup backs up the files in your Windows 7 libraries: Documents, Music, Pictures, and Video, as well as your favourites, contacts, e-mails, downloads, saved searches, and the contents of your desktop. Windows Backup also backs up the library files for the other users on your computer.

The Review Your Backup Settings dialog box appears.

⑪ Click **Save settings and run backup**.

If you are backing up to a CD or DVD, Windows Backup asks you to insert a blank disk.

⑫ Insert a blank disc in the drive.

⑬ Click **OK**.

Windows Backup asks if you are sure you want to format the disc.

**14** Click **Format**.

Windows Backup formats the disc and resumes the backup.

If the medium you are backing up to becomes full, the Label and Insert a Blank Media dialog box appears.

**15** Remove the full medium, replace it with a new one, and then click **OK**.

**Note:** *If your backup requires multiple media, you should give each medium a label, such as Backup 1, Backup 2, and so on.*

When the backup is done, the Windows Backup Has Completed Successfully dialog box appears.

**16** Click **Close**.

*By default, Windows Backup performs a weekly backup, which is fine for most users. To change the schedule, follow Steps 1 to 4, click Change settings, click Next, click Next, and then click Change schedule.*

199

# RESTORE BACKED-UP FILES

You can restore a file from a backup if the file is lost because your Windows 7 system crashed, or because the application you used to edit the file had some sort of problem and wrecked the file. You might also need to recover a file if you accidentally overwrote the file or if you deleted it and it was then removed from the Recycle Bin.

Even if you still have the file, you might want to recover an earlier version of it if you improperly edited the file by deleting or changing important data.

① Click **Start**.

② Click **All Programs**.

③ Click **Maintenance**.

④ Click **Backup and Restore**.

The Backup and Restore window appears.

⑤ Click **Restore my files**.

The Browse or Search Your Backup for Files and Folders to Restore dialog box appears.

⑥ If you backed up using a removable medium such as a CD, DVD, or memory card, insert the medium that contains the backups.

⑦ Click **Browse for files**.

Ⓐ *If you want to restore an entire folder, click **Browse for folders**, instead.*

The Browse the Backup for Files dialog box appears.

 Open the folder that contains the file you want to restore.

⑨ Click the file you want to restore.

**Note:** *To restore multiple files from the same folder, press and hold* **Ctrl** *and click each file.*

⑩ Click **Add files**.

Ⓐ *The file you selected appears in the list.*

⑪ Repeat Steps **7** to **10** to select other files to restore.

⑫ Click **Next**.

continued ➡

201

You can restore all of the backed-up files, which is useful after a major system crash. If you are having problems with or are missing just a few files, you can restore just those backed-up files.

You can also restore the files in their original locations or in a different location. Using a different location is useful if you want to preserve the existing version of a file. By restoring it to a different location, you get to work with both versions.

The Where Do You Want to Restore Your Files? dialog box appears.

**13** Click **In the original location** (◎ changes to ◉).

If you prefer to restore the file to another folder, click **In the following location** (◎ changes to ◉), instead, and then click **Browse** to choose the location.

**14** Click **Restore**.

If you do not have the correct backup media inserted, Windows Backup prompts you to insert the correct disc or drive.

**15** Insert the requested media.

**16** Click **OK**.

If a file with the same name exists in the original location, you see the Copy File dialog box.

17 If you want Windows Backup to handle all conflicts the same way, click **Do this for all conflicts** (☐ changes to ☑).

**18** Click **Copy and Replace**.

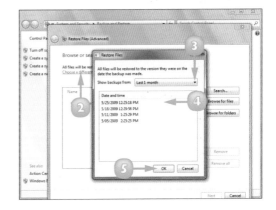

**A** *If you want to keep the original, click **Don't copy**, instead.*

**B** *If you want to see both files, click **Copy, but keep both files**, instead.*

The Your Files Have Been Restored dialog box appears.

**19** Click **Finish**.

## Restore from an Older Backup

**1** Follow Steps **1** to **5** to display the Browse or Search Your Backup for Files and Folders to Restore dialog box.

**2** Click **Choose a different date**.

**3** In the Restore Files dialog box, click the **Show backups from** ⊡ and then click the timeframe that includes the backup you want to work with.

**4** Click the backup.

**5** Click **OK**.

# INDEX

205

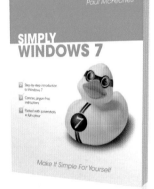